The Contemporary *Eruv*

Eruvin in Modern Metropolitan Areas

Rabbi Yosef Gavriel Bechhofer

ISBN 1-4196-4381-9

To order additional copies, please contact us.
BookSurge, LLC
www.booksurge.com
1-866-308-6235
orders@booksurge.com

TABLE OF CONTENTS

Chapter IV:

The Construction of Eruvin in Urban Areas

Chapter V:

Renting the Area from the Authorities and Eruvei Chatzeiros in Multiple Unit Dwellings and Hotels

ישיבת נר ישראל

NER ISRAEL RABBINICAL COLLEGE
400 MT. WILSON LANE
BALTIMORE, MARYLAND 21208

I was privileged to go through a Kuntres on "Eruvin in Modern Metropolitan Areas." The author is Ha'Rav Yosef Gavriel Bechhofer.

It was an informative and stimulating learning. The Halachos were presented with clarity and depth. The reasoning was strong and consistent; the conclusions justified and reliable as a whole.

Rav Bechhofer has a great zechus in presenting this Kuntres for the advancement of Torah and its observance among the many.

Rav Bechhofer, shlita has enhanced his previous work and made it even more useful and more complete. I have expressed my gratitude to him for an excellent presentation of a complex and important area of Jewish law.

Yaakov Weinberg

KOLEL AVRECHIM OF TORONTO

כולל אברכים דטאראנטא

INSTITUTE FOR ADVANCED TALMUDIC STUDY

315 COLDSTREAM AVENUE
TORONTO, ONTARIO M6B 2K7
416 - 789-5682 789-1853

בס"ד

הנה ידידי הנכבד הרב יוסף גבריאל בעכהאפער שליט"א
כתב קונטרס בענין בעיות הנולדות בתיקוני עירובין
וראיתי שדבריו נאמרים בטוב טעם ודעת ובלשון צח, ואין
מטרת הקונטרס לפסוק הלכות למעשה אלא להודיע הבעיות
והקושי בתיקוני עירובין. ודבר חשוב עשה שמצד חוסר הידיעה
בענינים של עירובין רבים נבוכים בהם ובעיני ראיתי עירובין
בכמה מקומות שלא היו כשרים ע"פ דת, וע"י רבוי הידיעה
וההשכלה ודאי יתוקן הרבה בשמירת שבת כדין וכהלכה
ולכן מברכו שיזכה להגדיל [illegible]

שלמה [illegible].

בס"ד

מש"כ בדף כ' סק ב לענין [illegible] במחיצה [illegible]
אודות מחיצות עירוב, הנה ועיקר הדין לא נאמר אלא
בפס' [illegible] ולא בדין מחיצות יש במקום [illegible] עירובין [illegible]

מש"כ בדף ח' [illegible]
[illegible]
[illegible]
[illegible]
[illegible]
[illegible]
[illegible]
[illegible]

FOREWORD

I am grateful to הקב"ה who caused the first, pamphlet editions of this work to find favor in the eyes of the public. Many people have remarked on the positive impact that the קונטרס had on the state of *eruvin* in עם ישראל.

This greatly expanded and revised full length (and renamed) edition includes new areas of inquiry. Specifically, the first two chapters: "The Restriction on Carrying and the *Eruv* Alternative" and "The Municipal *Eruv:* Its History and Evolution" are entirely new. The remaining three chapters also incorporate significant new sections.

I have also attempted to correct mistakes that occurred in the pamphlet editions and to clarify subjects that were either inaccurate or unclear in those editions. Nevertheless, the process of correction is imperfect, and it often leads, inadvertently, to additional errors. I will continue to appreciate any constructive criticism.

Although this work may be used for reference (and, for this purpose, it includes a list of references to סוגיות in *Messechtos Shabbos* and *Eruvin*), I mean it, primarily, to be read and studied, as the written equivalent of a series of שיעורים in *Hilchos Eruvin*. To this end, I have attempted to: a) use plain, uninterrupted English; and, b) to refrain from the use of distracting titles and descriptions, as much as possible: "למען ירוץ הקורא בו"- to allow the reader to pursue the work in a smooth, flowing manner. (Thus, the absence of titles such as *Ha'Ga'on* and descriptions such as *zt"l* and *shlita* is not meant, ח"ו, to diminish the great respect and deference that we all feel toward מרנן ורבנן גדולי התורה וההוראה אשר מפיהם אנו חיים but to facilitate readability.)

Many of the notes are integral components of this study, and I have attempted to compose them in a readable fashion as well. In quite a few instances, the division between text and note serves primarily to distinguish between material on a basic level and more in-depth analysis.

I am most thankful to my עזר כנגדו Shoshana Michal *shetichye,* whose patience and encouragement are always crucial in enabling my work on this and other Torah projects. May we see נחת from our children, and merit raising them לתורה לחופה ולמעשים טובים.

מודה אני להשי"ת אשר שם חלקי מיושבי בית המדרש.

אחת שאלתי מאת ה' אותה אבקש שבתי בבית ה' כל ימי חיי.

Yosef Gavriel Bechhofer

Adar 5758

Chicago, IL

ACKNOWLEDGMENTS

First and foremost, I would like to thank the גדולי התורה וההוראה who granted their הסכמות to this work.

I am grateful to the *Poskim* and *Rabbeim* who have instucted and guided me in *Inyanei Eruvin* (in order of my connection with them): Rabbi Moshe Brown, *Rosh Yeshiva* in *Yeshiva Derech Ayson* and מרא דאתרא of the *Agudas Yisroel* of West Lawrence, Far Rockaway, NY; Rabbi Moshe Dov Stein, *Posek* in *Yeshiva Shor Yoshuv*, Far Rockaway; Rabbi Dovid Zucker, *Rosh Ha'Kollel, Kollel Zichron Shneur*, Chicago, IL; Rabbi Chaim Twerski, *Rebbe* in *Yeshivas Beis HaMedrash LaTorah* and מרא דאתרא of the *Beis Medrash* of Lincolnwood, Lincolnwood, IL; and, Rabbi Ben Zion Wosner, אב"ד ומו"ץ of *Beis Horo'oh Shevet HaLevi*, Monsey, NY. I am also grateful to my *chevrusos* and חברים: Rabbi Menachem M. Blank; Rabbi Avrohom Yitzchok Berman; Rabbi Gershon Eliezer Schaffel; ואחרון אחרון חביב, the לומדים of the morning *Daf Yomi Shiur* at Cong. Bnei Ruven and the מתפללים of Cong. Bais Tefila, in Chicago.

I am most thankful to my mother, Mrs. Schulamith Bechhofer, who lovingly provided support and assistance in honor and in the זכות of the continued Torah growth and accomplishments of her children and grandchildren. I gratefully acknowledge the many people who read the pamphlet editions of this work and provided constructive criticism, most of which I incorporated in this edition. (Wherever possible, the תלמידי חכמים who provided me with insight and critique are acknowledged in the relevant notes. יישר חילם לאורייתא!) In particular I would like to thank my aunt, Mrs. Meta Bechhofer, who carefully proofread the work and enabled me to correct many typographical and stylistic errors therein. I am greatly indebted to my good friend, Rabbi Eliezer Lachman, of Baltimore, MD; and, to my distinguished cousin, Reb Emanuel Yosef Diena of Toronto, Ontario, for their assistance as well.

I owe הכרת הטוב to *Yeshivas Beis HaMedrash LaTorah*'s הנהלה and Board of Directors for all the תלמוד and הרבצת תורה they have enabled me to accomplish and, especially, for establishing and supporting the Frumi Noble Night Kollel. Many issues discussed in this קונטרס were first formulated in my שיעורים at the Night Kollel. I owe a special debt of gratitude to Rabbi Yitzchok Sender, one of the Yeshiva's *Roshei Yeshiva*, for his ongoing assistance and חיזוק.

I am grateful to the benefactors of the previous, pamphlet editions of this work: to Rabbi Jerome Lefton of St. Louis, MO; my father, Mr. Ernst Bechhofer of New Rochelle, NY; the Brandman and Atkin family of Chicago; and, Mr. Jack Saltzman, also of Chicago, who found those editions significant enough to warrant underwriting its publication. יישר חילם לאורייתא!

I thank Mrs. Sara Vitman of Sara Graphics of Chicago for her expert layout and illustrations outstanding.

I would like to conclude by expressing my deepest feelings of appreciation for Feldheim Publishers and, in particular, Mr. Yitzchok Feldheim, for undertaking the publication of this full length *sefer*. May their wonderful efforts for הרבצת תורה and כבוד שמים be blessed, always, with הצלחה, ברכה and נחת!

INTRODUCTION

Strictly speaking, the term *"eruv"* (plural: *eruvin*) is a misnomer. The word means "mixture," or, in this context, more precisely, "unification." In the Talmudic sources it refers to the symbolic amalgamation of all the residents in houses that surrounded a common courtyard via a commonly owned foodstuff. This unification allows those residents to carry from their houses into the courtyard and vice versa. (We will explore this concept and its details in Chapter I and again in Chapter V.) Although the word *eruv*, as we will use it, is a short form of the complete phrase *"eruvei chatzeiros,"* "unifications of courtyards" (*chatzer* = courtyard - plural: *chatzeiros*), it was originally unconnected to the enclosure of an area. (In the Talmud itself there are several types of *eruvin*: An *eruvei chatzeiros* allows carrying on *Shabbos*. An *eruv techumin* allows walking in one direction up to four thousand *amos* (cubits - singular: *amah* - see Chapter I, note 8 for measurements) - beyond the city limits, twice the normal maximum of two thousand *amos*. An *eruv tavshilin* allows preparations for *Shabbos* such as cooking to be performed on a *Yom Tov* that falls on a Friday. We call all these procedures *eruvin*. Presently, however, the generic use of the word *"eruv"* usually refers to an *eruvei chatzeiros*.) An area first is enclosed, then its residents engage in the *eruv* procedure, i.e., one of their number takes some bread or matzo and pronounces the proper blessing and formula.[1] They may then carry from their homes into the common area, and vice versa, and from home to home as well.

Indeed, the term *eruvei chatzeiros* only extends to houses, courtyards and the like. Carrying into, from, and within an area that encompasses streets (fig. 1, see overleaf) is allowed (following proper enclosure) by a similar procedure that goes under a different name: *"shitufei mevo'os,"* "partnership in streets" (*mavoi* = alley, or street - plural: *mevo'os*).

Nevertheless, colloquial usage has extended the use of the term *"eruv"* to include any reference to the enclosure that is a precondition

---

[1] See *Shemiras Shabbos K'Hilchasa*, 17:13:b.

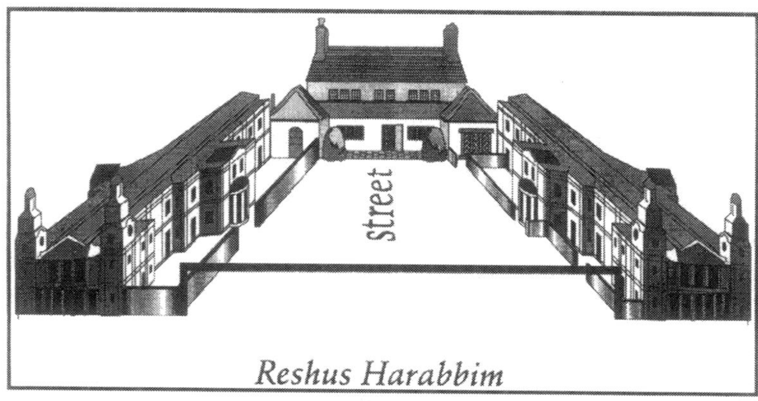

Fig. 1

for the *eruv* procedure. It seems that the current usage evolved in the following manner: As we will see (in our expanded discussion of the halachic background in Chapter I), the Torah forbids us to carry in any area defined as a *"reshus ha'rabbim"* (a public domain - plural: *reshuyos ha'rabbim*) on *Shabbos*. *Chazal* (the Sages) extended this prohibition to include any unenclosed area.[2]

For thousands of years, however, cities were generally surrounded by walls. While there were concerns about breaks in the walls and gateways, since a typical city was essentially enclosed, little preliminary work was necessary. Thus, to enable themselves to carry within a city, the Jewish residents of a city needed only to rent the right to carry from the authorities (*"sechiras reshus"* - a procedure that we will explain in Chapter V), and perform the *eruv* or *shituf* procedure.

In modern times, however, older cities outgrew their walls. Newer

---

[2] In our discussion of the issues surrounding contemporary *eruvin* we will frequently encounter distinctions between laws that are of Torah origin - *me'd'oraysa* - and laws that are of rabbinic origin - *me'd'rabbanan*. As we will see, the entire concept of an *eruv* based on *tzuras ha'pesach* is predicated on the assumption that our streets are not true *reshuyos ha'rabbim*, and that, therefore, the prohibition to carry to, from and within them is only *me'd'rabbanan*. We will expand the discussion on this point in Chapter I.

cities were built without walls altogether. As we will see (in our overview of the history of municipal *eruvin* in Chapter II), halachic authorities were then forced to grapple with the challenge of effectively enclosing a city in a way that would be acceptable to the civil authorities. The least obtrusive and most economical halachic method of enclosing an area is a *"tzuras ha'pesach"* (literally: the form of a doorway - the familiar two poles with a wire across the top and the variations on that theme - the parameters of which we will discuss in detail in Chapter IV - plural: *tzuros ha'pesach.*). The rationale of this solution is that a door frame is a halachically valid form of enclosure.[3] The invention of the telegraph and telephone and the resulting proliferation of poles and wires in metropolitan areas made this method especially prevalent and expedient.

Over time, the term *eruv* came to refer more to this method of enclosure than to the actual *eruv* procedure. *Eruvin* of this sort enclose areas as small as a backyard and as large as entire neighborhoods or cities.

Often, the construction of an *eruv* in an urban setting becomes a matter of controversy. Almost inevitably, the issues involved in the controversy cause much confusion and strife, especially among those unfamiliar with the Halachos of *eruvin*. The focus of such controversies usually centers on the halachic definition of a *reshus ha'rabbim*, i.e., what constitutes a public domain that cannot be halachically enclosed with the device of *tzuras ha'pesach*. A common misconception is that once the *reshus ha'rabbim* question is resolved, the actual construction of the *eruv* is a simple and straightforward matter. The *Chazon Ish*, however, is alleged to have remarked that he never saw a city with a *"pasul* [invalid] *mikvah"* (due to all the stringencies that we implement when building a *mikvah)* or a *"kosher* [valid] *eruv"* (due to the intricate details involved in the construction of a valid enclosure that may be overlooked). Most of the problems in contemporary *eruvin* occur in the sphere of construction.

There are three major areas of concern in dealing with contemporary *eruvin*:

---

[3] *Eruvin* 11b.

1) The *reshus ha'rabbim* issue. We will deal with this issue in Chapter III.

2) Problems in the construction of urban *eruvin*. This issue is the focus of Chapter IV.

3) How to go about renting the area in question from the authorities. (This area will lead us to explore the additional contemporary concerns of *eruvei chatzeiros* in apartment buildings and hotels.) We will come to this issue in Chapter V.

This work is in no way intended to decide practical Halacha. It is intended to educate and alert: a) persons involved in the construction and maintenance of *eruvin*; and, b) the public that uses *eruvin*, to <u>some</u> possible problems and issues they may face.[4] Any actual question should be submitted to an authority in the Halachos of *eruvin* for a practical ruling.

A caveat: An argument that frequently appears in literature concerning *eruvin* is that it is worthwhile building *eruvin* - even if they must rely on extraordinary leniencies and *dei'os yachid* (an opinion expressed by a single authority, but rejected by most of the authorities that deal with the issue) - to save ignorant Jews who may be unaware of the prohibition of *Hotza'a* from a severe sin.[5] This is not the place to discuss the halachic and philosophical issues

---

[4] An often misapplied principle is that of: *"Halacha k'divrei hameykeil b'eruv"* (the Halacha, in an argument concerning matters of *eruv*, follows the more lenient opinion - *Eruvin* 46a). Some modern authorities even extend this principle to the point of using it to support their own lenient rulings! (See *No'am* vol. 1 pp. 214-215 and Rabbi Ya'akov Yeshaya Blau's *Nesivos Shabbos* (Yerushalayim, 1989) 15:2 and notes 4-5 for a list of sources that deal with this principle and summaries of their opinions.) The *Chazon Ish, Orach Chaim,* 112:10, proves that this principle does not apply to later authorities. Whenever we deal with an issue discussed by the *Acharonim* (authorities subsequent to the redaction of the *Shulchan Aruch*) we follow a weighted majority opinion. We must weigh the stature and reasoning of each rabbinic authority when considering his views and counting his ruling in the halachic equation. See also Rabbi Shlomo Miller's note on this point in his *haskama* to this work.

[5] See, for example, Rabbi Yosef Moskowitz' *Kuntres Tikunei Eruvin of Manhattan* (New York, 1959) pp. 161-164.

involved in such an approach. If, however, this approach is utilized and implemented in building an *eruv*, it is essential to clarify to the observant residents of the enclosed area that extraordinary leniencies were employed in making the *eruv* there a reality, and that they should, therefore, continue to refrain from carrying within that *eruv*.[6]

---

6 We will focus in this work on the halachic issues surrounding *eruvin* in modern metropolitan areas. It would be remiss, however, not to note the extensive philosophical and theological conflicts that surrounded the construction of *eruvin* in several major metropolitan areas. These conflicts centered on what would, ultimately, serve the greater good of *Shabbos* observance in the North American milieu: Allowing or disallowing carrying in public on *Shabbos*. Some of this discussion focuses on the reasons why the Sages - as is evident from many Talmudic sources - did not put a city-wide *eruv* into effect in Yerushalayim (see *Igros Moshe, Orach Chaim*, 1:139-140 and *No'am*, vol. 1, pp. 238-244).

Passionate arguments against the construction of urban *eruvin* were mustered by Rabbi Shimon Schwab in *HaPardes* 36:5. He reprinted that essay in his *Ma'ayan Beis HaSho'eivah* (New York, 1994), pp. 231-234, accompanied by a 1962 proclamation that forbade the construction of *eruvin* in large cities (referred to in *Igros Moshe, Orach Chaim*, vol. 4, p. 428). Nevertheless, signatories of that proclamation subsequently allowed the construction of *eruvin* in major metropolitan areas, if they met certain criteria that they imposed (see below, Chapter III, Section 3).

It is not our intent to address these issues, pivotal and important as they are. The reality is that most major metropolitan areas in North America include extensive *eruvin*. Many rabbinic authorities forbid those who follow their guidance to use those *eruvin*. On the other hand, however, many rabbinic authorities permit, even encourage, both the construction of new *eruvin* and the use of extant *eruvin* in their communities.

Many of these *eruvin* were and are constructed by great experts and authorities, the leading *Poskim* (authoritative halachic decisors - singular: *Posek*) on this continent both yesterday and today. Many, however, were, and are, not. It is my fervent hope that this work will serve: a) To help clarify "benchmark" standards of *eruvin*; b) To allow both local rabbinates and laities to understand, address, resolve and correct issues and problems; and, c) To enhance the collective preservation and observance of *Shabbos* in communities across the continent. I pray to *HaKadosh Baruch Hu* that this work may generate progress toward these goals, in accordance with His will.

Chapter I

THE RESTRICTION ON CARRYING AND THE ERUV ALTERNATIVE

1. D'Oraysa (the Torah Itself) and D'Rabbanan (Enacted by the Sages)

One of the primary activities prohibited on *Shabbos* and *Yom Tov*[7] is *"Hotza'a"* - transferring or carrying an object. On a *d'oraysa* level (forbidden by the Torah itself) this prohibition has two manifestations:

1. One may not carry an object from a private domain (a *"reshus ha'yachid"*) into a public domain (a *"reshus ha'rabbim"*) and vice versa.
2. One may not carry an object for a distance of four *amos*[8] or more within a *reshus ha'rabbim*.

There are many additional restrictions involved in the prohibition of *"Hotza'a"* - carrying or transferring objects on *Shabbos* - that are *d'rabbanan*, rabbinic in origin. The Talmud therefore severely admonishes us (free translation):[9]

> Rava pronounced: What is the meaning of the verse: "And more than those, my son, be cautious of the making of many

[7] On *Yom Tov*, any carrying for the purpose of enhancing the *Yom Tov* - even in a very minor way (*"l'tzorech ktzas"*) - is permitted. Only carrying for purposes entirely unrelated to *Yom Tov* is forbidden. See *Shulchan Aruch, Orach Chaim* 518:1.

[8] There are two major opinions on the measurement of an *amah*. One school of thought, that identified with Rabbi Avrohom Chaim Na'eh, holds an *amah* to be approximately eighteen inches, or, exactly, 48 centimeters. The other school, identified with the *Chazon Ish*, holds an *amah* to be about two feet, or, exactly, 57.6 centimeters.

[9] *Eruvin* 21b.

books" etc.?[10] It means: "My son, be more cautious in matters enacted by the Sages than in matters enacted by the Torah itself," for some enactments of the Torah are positive commandments, and some are negative commandments [i.e., there are varying degrees of severity], but as to the enactments of the Sages, anyone who transgresses the enactments of the Sages is subject to capital punishment [at the hands of G-d]. If you wonder why, if they [the Sages' enactments] are so significant, are they not included in the Torah itself? The verse continues and responds: "The making of many books without end" [i.e., there are so many enactments that including them in the Torah itself would have undermined its terse and concise format].

The *Gemara* then continues in this vein, stressing the significance and severity of rabbinic enactments. Farther down on the same page, the *Gemara* relates:

> Rav Yehuda said in the name of Shmuel: When King Solomon enacted the laws of *Eruvin* and *Netilas Yadayim* [washing one's hands before eating], a heavenly voice came forth and said: "My son, if your heart is wise, my heart will rejoice as well."[11] It also says [it is unclear whether Shmuel is asserting that this, too, was part of the pronouncement from Heaven, or whether he is simply citing a parallel reference]: "Be wise, my son, and gladden my heart, then I can respond to those who mock me."[12]

At the very end of the page, the *Gemara* relates:

> Ulla said in the name of Rabbi Elazar: Initially the Torah was like a basket that has no handles; then King Solomon

---

[10] *Koheles* 12:2.

[11] *Mishlei* 23:15.

[12] Ibid., 27:11. It seems that Shmuel intended to interpret this latter verse to connote that the prevalence of additional enactments that the Jewish people - here, King Solomon - accept upon themselves, is a phenomenon that shows our devotion to G-d, and is therefore a source of pride for Him.

came and fashioned for it handles.

Rashi explains that just as it is easier to grasp a basket with handles than one that has none, so too King Solomon's enactments, including the two cited by Shmuel, allow us to strengthen our grip on *mitzvos* by distancing us from potential transgressions.

The precise extent of King Solomon's enactment concerning *eruvin* is described by *Rashi* elsewhere,[13] and by the *Rambam* as well:[14]

> The Torah itself allows the residents of a courtyard in which many neighbors reside - each in his own home - to carry [objects on *Shabbos*] throughout the courtyard, from the homes into the courtyard and vice versa, because the courtyard [and all the houses are] all *reshus ha'yachid*. The same is true of a street[15] [walled on three sides] that possesses a post or beam [on the fourth side]:[16] All those who reside along that street may carry throughout it, from the courtyards to the street and vice versa, because the street [together with all the courtyards along it - with the houses that open into them - are] all *reshus ha'yachid*. The same is true of a district enclosed by a wall that is ten *tefachim*[17] high whose doors are closed at night: It is all *reshus ha'yachid*. All this is Torah law.
>
> The Sages, however, forbade neighbors to carry, even within one *reshus ha'yachid*, from and into separate homes,

---

[13] *Shabbos* 6b *d.h. Lo Eerev* and 14b *d.h. Eruvin*. See below, note 20.

[14] *Mishne Torah, Hilchos Eruvin* 1:1-6.

[15] The literal translation of the Hebrew term used here: "*mavoi*" is "alley." Since, however, there is generally no distinction in Halacha between a street and an alley, we will use the more prevalent term.

[16] The *Rambam*'s opinion is that the definition of a *reshus ha'yachid me'd'oraysa* is an area enclosed in some manner on all four sides. Most other *Rishonim* disagree - see below, note 24.

[17] See below, note 22.

unless all the neighbors participate in an *eruv* before *Shabbos* commences. This law applies equally to courtyards, to streets and to districts. Solomon and his court promulgated this regulation.

Even individuals camped in tents, huts or any other type of encampment surrounded by a fence may not carry from tent to tent unless they all participate in an *eruv*. Travelers in a caravan that has pitched camp for *Shabbos* and enclosed itself in a fence, however, do not need an *eruv*, and they may carry freely from tent to tent. This is because their mutual participation in a caravan is already an *eruv*, while their temporary encampment in separate tents does not render them separate.

Why did Solomon promulgate this regulation? So that people should not erroneously assume that just as they are allowed to carry from the courtyards of a district to its streets and marketplaces, so, too, are they allowed to carry from the [enclosed] district to the fields[18] and vice versa. In other words, were people allowed to carry freely in streets and marketplaces [in an enclosed area], they might mistakenly infer that if they are allowed to carry in these domains that are accessible to all, so may they carry to fields and deserts[19] that are similarly accessible to all. They would also [logically - but erroneously -] reason: a) Only courtyards are true *reshuyos ha'yachid*. b) One is allowed to carry from these *reshuyos ha'yachid* to streets and marketplace. c) It follows [again, logically - but erroneously -] that since streets and marketplaces [where carrying is allowed] are similar in nature to fields and deserts [carrying must, therefore, be allowed there as well. People would have thus come to the gravely mistaken conclusion that] there is no prohibition on *Hotza'a*,

[18] The commentators note that the *Rambam's* use of the word "fields" is somewhat difficult, as in *Hilchos Shabbos* 14:4 the *Rambam* classified fields as *carmelis*. Perhaps the *Rambam* means that the highways leading to the field are *reshuyos ha'rabbim*.

[19] The *Rambam* in *Hilchos Shabbos* 14:1 classified deserts as *reshuyos ha'rabbim*.

i.e., that one may carry and transfer objects from a *reshus ha'yachid* to a *reshus ha'rabbim*.

He [Solomon] therefore enacted: In any case that a *reshus ha'yachid* shared by residents that live in separate homes retains a common area that is equally accessible to all those residents of the *reshus ha'yachid* - such as a courtyard that services several homes - that common area is regarded as if it were *reshus ha'rabbim*, while the surrounding homes are regarded as distinct *reshuyos ha'yachid*. Therefore, just as one may not carry from a *reshus ha'yachid* to a *reshus ha'rabbim*, it is forbidden to carry from the various homes to the common area. The residents may only use their own respective shares - even though they are all part of one large *reshus ha'yachid* [*me'd'oraysa*] - unless they join in an *eruv*.[20]

And what is this "*eruv*?" It is the unification of all the residents by means of a foodstuff that they designate from before the onset of *Shabbos*. By the possession of this food in common, they convey that they are all unified, and that no one of them should be considered separate from his counterparts. Rather, just as they are unified in this place [where the designated food is kept] they are unified in all the domains that each of them possesses, and they all comprise one domain. [The prevalence of] this procedure will prevent people from mistakenly assuming that they are freely allowed to carry and transfer objects from a *reshus ha'yachid* to a *reshus ha'rabbim*.

[20] The *Rambam*'s position is that an *eruv* is only required among neighbors that maintain a common area in which they are partners. *Rashi*, in the two places cited previously in note 13, states explicitly that King Solomon's decree forbade transferring objects from any individual's *reshus ha'yachid* to any other individual's *reshus ha'yachid* regardless of whether they maintain some area in common (without an *eruv*). Most *Poskim* reject the *Rambam*'s opinion in this regard, and the *Shulchan Aruch, Orach Chaim* 372:5 requires an *eruv* to permit the transfer of objects between adjacent houses regardless of whether they maintain a common area. The *Avnei Nezer, Orach Chaim* 1:301, attempts to reconcile the position of the *Rambam* with that of *Rashi*, asserting that the *Rambam* agrees that carrying between any two *reshuyos ha'yachid* without an *eruv* is prohibited, and that he differs in another scenario.

The *eruv* that residents of a courtyard contract with each other is called *"eruvei chatzeiros,"* while that which residents of a street or of a district contract with each other is called *"shitufei mevo'os."*

2. *The Parameters of the Prohibition of Hotza'ah*

The precise parameters of the prohibition of *Hotza'a* involve many details and regulations. A thorough discussion of those parameters is beyond the scope of our deliberations. Extensive reviews of the issue may be found in many works on the topic. We must, however, know more about the framework of these laws and their functions before proceeding to analyze contemporary *eruvin*.

We can learn much additional background material by studying the *Tur*.[21] Not all of the following material is absolutely essential for our purposes. Some of it addresses the broader framework of the parameters of the prohibition to carry between and within various domains. Nevertheless, it is hard to sort out what is necessary and what is not. Besides, in this area, a little more knowledge can only help!

There are four domains that pertain to *Shabbos*: *Reshus ha'yachid, reshus ha'rabbim, carmelis* and *makom patur.*

A *reshus ha'yachid* is an area enclosed by walls that are at least ten *tefachim*[22] high. The size of the area must be at

[21] *Orach Chaim* 345-346. True, the *Tur*, a fourteenth century codification of all major areas of Jewish Law relevant to diaspora Jewry written by Rabbi Ya'akov, son of the *"Rosh,"* Rabbi Asher, is not the final word in areas of Halacha. Rabbi Yosef Karo's sixteenth century *Shulchan Aruch* (coupled with the *"Mapa"* - the glosses of the *Rama*, Rabbi Moshe Isserles) bears that distinction. Nevertheless, it is more instructive, for our purposes, to peruse the more verbose and detailed *Tur*, rather than the more terse and decisive *Shulchan Aruch* (Rabbi Karo traces the *Tur's* sources and lays out his disputes with the *Tur's* conclusions in his comprehensive commentary on the *Tur*, the *"Beis Yosef"*). A review of the *Tur* is a convenient way to gain familiarity with basic concepts drawn from a vast array of Talmudic and medieval sources. Outstanding illustrations of many of the concepts discussed by the *Tur* can be found in the *Arba'ah Turim HaShalem* (Yerushalayim, 1993), vol. 4, in the back of the volume.

[22] There are six *tefachim* in an *amah*. Thus, according to Rabbi Avrohom Chaim Na'eh,

least four by four *tefachim*. A *reshus ha'yachid* may, however, extend several miles in each direction, if its perimeter was [originally] enclosed for the purpose of habitation and its doors are closed at night. An animal pen or corral, even a trench that is ten *tefachim* deep and four by four *tefachim* in area at its bottom, or a mound that is ten *tefachim* high and four by four *tefachim* in area at its top, are all *reshuyos ha'yachid*.

Both the tops of, and the nooks in, the walls surrounding a *reshus ha'yachid* are part of that *reshus ha'yachid*.

The airspace of a *reshus ha'yachid* is part of that *reshus ha'yachid*.

Even a movable object such as a box, a beehive or portable closet, is a *reshus ha'yachid* if it is ten *tefachim* high and four by four *tefachim* in area.

A *reshus ha'rabbim* is a street or marketplace that is: a) at least sixteen *amos* wide by sixteen *amos* long; b) that runs in an uninterrupted line from one gate of the city to another gate of the city; and, c) that six hundred thousand people traverse.

Any object present in a *reshus ha'rabbim* that is not three *tefachim* high is considered part of the surface of the *reshus ha'rabbim*. This is true even if the object is one that people avoid stepping upon, such as thorns or excrement. If the object is between three and nine *tefachim* in height and four by four *tefachim* in area, it is a *carmelis*. If it is less than four by four *tefachim*, then it is a *makom patur*. If the object is between nine and ten *tefachim* high and people make use of its top to shoulder their loads, then it is part of the *reshus ha'rabbim* - even if it is less than four by four *tefachim* in area.

---

ten *tefachim* equal slightly more than 30 inches (*tefach* - about three inches, exactly eight centimeters); according to the *Chazon Ish*, slightly lower than 40 inches (*tefach* - about four inches, exactly 9.6 centimeters). See *Shemiras Shabbos K'Hilchasa* p. 11.

An object in a *reshus ha'rabbim* that is ten or more *tefachim* high and four by four *tefachim* in area is a *reshus ha'yachid*. If the object is less than four by four *tefachim*, it is a *makom patur* - even if it is large enough that a four by four surface could be hewed in it somewhere beneath the height of ten *tefachim*.

A hole in a *reshus ha'rabbim* that is shallower than three *tefachim* is part of the *reshus ha'rabbim*. If the hole is between three and ten *tefachim* in depth and is also four by four *tefachim* in area, it is a *carmelis*. If it is less than four by four *tefachim*, then it is a *makom patur*.

The airspace above a *reshus ha'rabbim* is only part of the *reshus ha'rabbim* up to the height of ten *tefachim*. The airspace above ten *tefachim* is a *makom patur*.

A hole in a wall that abuts a *reshus ha'rabbim* is not included in the *reshus ha'rabbim*. Its definition depends on its dimensions. If it is four by four *tefachim* in area and ten *tefachim* high, it is a *reshus ha'yachid*. If it is four by four *tefachim* in area but not ten *tefachim* high, it is a *carmelis*. If the hole is smaller in area than four by four *tefachim*, but more than three *tefachim* above the ground, it is a *makom patur*.

A *carmelis* is a place that is not intended to serve as a thoroughfare for masses. Examples of *carmelis* include a lake [or sea], an area encompassing many cultivated fields, areas [in front of stores that line a *reshus ha'rabbim*] designated for storekeepers to sit in, areas [designated for peddlers to hang their wares] between pillars that interrupt a *reshus ha'rabbim*, the raised platforms surrounding those pillars [designated for peddlers to sit upon], and streets that come off a *reshus ha'rabbim* at an angle. [This category] includes streets[23] surrounded by three walls that do not possess a post or beam on the fourth side [to set them off from the adjacent *reshus*

[23] See above, note 15.

ha'rabbim].[24] [Other categories of *carmelis*] include a *reshus ha'rabbim* that has been roofed over, an area completely enclosed by walls that are not ten *tefachim* high, mounds that are four by four *tefachim* in area, but not ten *tefachim* high, and trenches that are four by four *tefachim* in area but not ten *tefachim* deep.

A house that is: a) four by four *tefachim* in area; b) shorter than ten *tefachim* in height internally; but, c) higher then ten *tefachim* externally because of the additional height of its roof, is a *carmelis* within its roof and under its ceiling, but a *reshus ha'yachid* atop its roof. If, however, in some part of the house there is a depression that is at least four by four *tefachim* in area, from which there are ten *tefachim* to the ceiling, then the entire inside of the house is a *reshus ha'yachid*.

A roof that extends beyond the walls of the house

---

[24] The *Rambam, Hilchos Shabbos* 14:4, holds that an area enclosed on three of its four sides is a *carmelis me'd'oraysa* (according to Torah law). *Me'd'oraysa* there are only three domains. (We will see shortly that the Torah draws no distinction between a *makom patur* and a *carmelis*. The Torah itself prohibits: a) carrying from a *reshus ha'rabbim* into a *reshus ha'yachid* and vice versa; and, b) carrying an object four *amos* within a *reshus ha'rabbim*. Carrying into either *reshus* from a *carmelis* and vice versa, and carrying four *amos* within a *carmelis* are rabbinic prohibitions.)

Most other *Rishonim* (medieval authorities) hold that the presence of three walls renders an enclosed area a *reshus ha'yachid me'd'oraysa*, but that the Rabbis "downgraded" the status of the enclosed area to that of a *carmelis*, barring one from carrying within the enclosure unless some halachically valid wall-like structure, or at least a reminder - such as the post or beam mentioned here - not to carry further, is constructed or positioned on the fourth side of the enclosed area (see *Maggid Mishne, Hilchos Shabbos* 17:9). It is not clear to which opinion the *Tur* subscribes (see *Aruch HaShulchan* here *se'if* 40 and *Arba'ah Turim HaShalem* here, *Hagohos v'He'aros* note 34). See *Biur Halacha* 363:1, *d.h. Asra Chachamim*.

These differences in theory are, generally, not relevant to practice. The "bottom line" is universal: The Sages required the residents of a street that is closed on three sides to build a post or beam on the fourth side to allow carrying within that street. If the street is open on two sides, then it does not suffice to build a beam or post on both ends. At least one side must be closed with a halachic wall such as a *tzuras ha'pesach*. See *Shulchan Aruch, Orach Chaim* 364:1 for details of (and exceptions to) this rule.

underneath it - so that the walls of the house are not visible to someone standing on that roof - is a *carmelis* - even if the roof is very high and broad. If, however, an opening [that is at least four by four *tefachim* in size][25] opens from the house below onto the roof, then the roof is a *reshus ha'yachid.* Similarly, a platform four by four *tefachim* in area that juts out from the wall of a house is a *carmelis* unless an opening from the house leads to it.

A hole in a wall that abuts a *carmelis* is not included in the *carmelis.*

The airspace of a *carmelis* only extends ten *tefachim* above its surface. The airspace higher than ten *tefachim* is a *makom patur.* In the case of an object floating on the waters of a lake or river, the first ten *tefachim* above the water are still a *carmelis;* the airspace above that is a *makom patur.*[26]

A well within a *carmelis* is a *carmelis* - even if it is one hundred *amos* deep - unless the well is four by four *tefachim* in area [in which case it is a *reshus ha'yachid*].[27]

A *makom patur* is either: a) an object that is not four by four *tefachim* in area, yet is higher than three *tefachim* above the ground (even as high as the sky); or, b) a trench that is not

---

[25] The *Beis Yosef* adds this parameter on the basis of the ruling of the *Rosh.*

[26] The *Beis Yosef* explains why the *Tur* brings this specific example. There is a disagreement in *Shabbos* 100b whether the ten *tefachim* of the *carmelis* begin from the bed of the lake or river or from the water's surface. The *Tur* meant to clarify that we follow the opinion of Rav Chisda and Rabba bar Rav Huna that the measurement begins from the water's surface.

[27] The comment within the brackets is made by the *Beis Yosef.* The *Beis Yosef* notes that while we have already seen that a trench in a *reshus ha'rabbim* that is less than four by four *tefachim* in area is considered a *makom patur;* when, however, that same type of trench is within a *carmelis,* it acquires the more stringent parameter of the surrounding *carmelis.* This phenomenon reflects the principle of *"matza min es mino"* (literally: "a kind finds its kindred kind"), i.e., the similarity between *carmelis* and *makom patur* is so great that the surrounding *carmelis* assimilates the *makom patur.*

four by four *tefachim* in area, but is deeper than three *tefachim* beneath the ground. Similarly, if walls higher than three *tefachim* above the ground enclose an area that is less than four by four *tefachim* in size, even if that area is very long [and narrow],[28] it is a *makom patur*.[29]

The Torah itself only forbids removing, bringing, throwing and extending objects from a *reshus ha'rabbim* into a *reshus ha'yachid* and vice versa. The Sages expanded these prohibitions to include engaging in any of these activities from a *reshus ha'yachid* or a *reshus ha'rabbim* to a *carmelis* and vice versa. It is permissible, however, to remove or bring objects from anything defined as a *makom patur* to a *reshus ha'yachid* or a *reshus ha'rabbim* or vice versa. One is not allowed, however, to remove an object from a *reshus ha'yachid*, bring it into a *makom patur*, and then transfer it through the *makom patur* to a *reshus ha'rabbim* or vice versa. If one stands in a *reshus ha'yachid* and removes, brings, extends or throws an object into a *reshus ha'rabbim* via a *makom patur* or vice versa, one transgresses a Torah

---

[28] The *Beis Yosef*, based on the *Rambam*, ibid., 14:7, explains that it is not sufficient for a *reshus ha'yachid* to contain sixteen square *tefachim*. There must be some place in the *reshus ha'yachid* where we may describe an actual square of four by four *tefachim*. Thus, for example, an enclosure in the shape of a circle that contains an area of sixteen square *tefachim* would not be a *reshus ha'yachid*. The circle would have to be large enough to contain a square of four by four *tefachim*. The *Gemara* in *Sukka* 8a rules that 1.4 is a sufficient approximation of the square root of two and that three is a sufficient approximation of pi. In order, therefore, to constitute a *reshus ha'yachid*, the minimum radius of the circle would have to be approximately 2.8 *tefachim* and its area a little less than 24 square *tefachim*.

[29] The *Bayis Chadash* (the other major commentary on the *Tur*, by Rabbi Yoel Sirkes, commonly known by the acronym "*Bach*") notes that in light of the *Tur*'s previous ruling it seems that these parameters of *makom patur* only apply to an object or trench in a *reshus ha'rabbim*, while in a *carmelis* we would apply the principle of "*matza min es mino*" that we discussed in note 27. As the *Bach* himself notes, others disagree and draw a distinction between trenches - that are assimilated into the surrounding *carmelis*; and outcroppings and objects - that are not. See *Arba'ah Turim HaShalem, Hagohos v'He'aros* note 43.

prohibition.[30] Similarly, one may not position oneself in a *makom patur* in order to take objects from an individual in a *reshus ha'rabbim* and give them to a third party in a *reshus ha'yachid* or vice versa. Even if the *makom patur* is located between two domains between which it is only rabbinically forbidden to transfer objects, such as two yards that have not joined in a common *eruv*, one may not stand in that *makom patur* and transport objects from yard to yard - if those objects originated or will terminate in one of the houses fronting on the respective yards.[31]

---

[30] To understand these rulings, we must explore some background material:

As explained in the *Shulchan Aruch, Orach Chaim* 347:1 and the *Mishna Berura* there 347:2, the prohibition of transferring an object from one domain to another consists of three components: "*Akira*" - "uprooting" the object from its prior location; "*Hotza'a*" - moving the object from a prior domain to a subsequent one; and, "*Hanacha*" - the placement of the object in its subsequent location. *Akira* and *hanacha* do not require that one manually lift an object or set it down. For example, if: a) someone placed an object in your pocket while you were standing still; b) then, you went on to walk from the *reshus* in which you were standing into another domain; and, b) you then stood still again - never having touched the object in your pocket - you, nevertheless, transgressed the Torah's prohibition. The principle underlying this phenomenon is that "uprooting" your body (upon which the object may be found) from a stationary position and then "placing" your body in a stationary position are both tantamount, respectively, to uprooting and setting down the object itself.

If, however, you were to pick up an object in a *reshus ha'yachid* (or, if it were placed upon you while you were stationary), walk into a *makom patur*, and place the object (or, just halt) there - for even a brief moment - while you have completed all three components of the act of *hotza'a*, you are, nevertheless, exempt from any prohibition. To resume walking and enter a *reshus ha'rabbim* would be a new act of *hotza'a* - one for which you cannot be faulted with any Torah prohibition, as the second *akira* was performed in an exempt area - the *makom patur*. (You will, however, transgress a rabbinic ordinance, as noted here by the *Tur*.)

Were you not to stop in the *makom patur*, however, but rather walk (with the object) from a *reshus ha'yachid* through a *makom patur* into a *reshus ha'rabbim*, then the fact that you traversed a *makom patur* is irrelevant: If no *hanacha* takes place in the *makom patur*, it does not become a factor in defining this act. From an halachic perspective you have completed an *akira* in a *reshus ha'yachid*, *hotza'a*, and a *hanacha* in *reshus ha'rabbim* - a complete act that transgresses the Torah's parameters of prohibition.

[31] The *Tur* adds "the houses fronting on the respective yards" because there is no

The Torah itself only forbids carrying an object four *amos* in a *reshus ha'rabbim*. The Sages forbade one to carry an object four *amos* in a *carmelis*, lest one come to carry in a *reshus ha'rabbim*.

A *karpaf*[32] larger than a *beis se'asayim* [5000 square *amos* in any shape] that was not enclosed with the intent to render the area suitable for habitation[33] is, nevertheless, considered a *reshus ha'yachid me'd'oraysa*. The Sages, however, banned one from carrying an object four *amos* within such a *karpaf*, lest one come to carry in a *reshus ha'rabbim*. Nevertheless, it is permissible to transfer an object from a *karpaf* to another type of *carmelis* next to the *karpaf*, such as to an area encompassing many cultivated fields. This is permitted even though the *karpaf* is technically a *reshus ha'yachid me'd'oraysa* [while the area encompassing many cultivated fields is a *carmelis me'd'oraysa*]. Although the Sages generally forbade transferring objects from a *reshus ha'yachid* to a *carmelis*, in this case they allowed such activity, for were they to ban it, people might mistakenly conclude that a *karpaf* is a *reshus ha'yachid* even *me'd'rabbanan*, and would therefore come to carry objects within the *karpaf* indiscriminately. It was therefore deemed better to permit the relatively uncommon activity of transferring objects from a *karpaf* to a *carmelis* - so as to bolster the prohibition of carrying within the *karpaf* - than to prohibit that activity, lest people then [mistakenly] allow themselves to engage in the far more common activity of

---

prohibition to transfer objects that have been in one yard since before the onset of *Shabbos* to an adjacent yard where they will remain until after *Shabbos*, even if a common *eruv* does not connect them (*Shulchan Aruch*, ibid., 372:1). The prohibition of carrying without an *eruv* from yard to yard only applies to objects that were or will be inside one of the houses at some point during the course of the ensuing *Shabbos*.

[32] An area that is surrounded by an enclosure and not roofed over, similar in appearance to a courtyard (*Rama, Shulchan Aruch*, ibid., 346:3).

[33] The definition of suitable for "habitation" is rather broad. We shall discuss the issue in greater detail in Chapter IV, Section 7.

carrying objects within the *karpaf.* This, in turn, could lead people to carry in an actual *reshus ha'rabbim.* Therefore, if a walled garden larger than a *beis se'asayim* not designated for habitation adjoins an area encompassing many cultivated fields, it is permissible to take a key from that adjacent area, open the door to the garden, and place the key within the garden.

3. *Applications to Contemporary Urban Eruvin*

From all these parameters we may conclude that contemporary urban *eruvin* involve at least three stages of concern and activity:

1. To even consider the construction of an *eruv* based on *tzuras ha'pesach,* it must first be verified that there are no thoroughfares that may constitute a *reshus ha'rabbim* within the area under consideration. If any *reshus ha'rabbim* is located within the confines of an *eruv,* then doors that are suitable for closing at night must be installed on the *eruv's* perimeter to close each of those *reshuyos ha'rabbim.*[34]

2. After verifying that the area is not a *reshus ha'rabbim,* but a *carmelis,* it must be completely enclosed so as to render it a *reshus ha'yachid me'd'oraysa.* This enclosed area may not include any *karpeifos.*

3. Finally, after an effective enclosure has been achieved, an *eruv chatzeiros* and/or *shituf mevo'os* procedure must be performed.

[34] The extent to which such doors must actually be closed is a subject of great controversy. We will touch on the issue in Chapter IV, Section 8. It is very important to note that although we are generally entitled to rely on legitimate lenient opinions in *Hilchos Eruvin,* that is because once we have resolved (i.e., eliminated) the *reshus ha'rabbim* issue) there are no questions of *d'oraysa* involved, only questions of *d'rabbanan,* in which we are taught to be lenient ("*safek d'rabbanan l'kulla*"). If, however, there is an area that may be a *reshus ha'rabbim* in an *Eruv,* then there is a potential Torah prohibition of *hotza'a* involved. In cases where a *d'oraysa* may be involved, we are taught to be stringent ("*safek d'oraysa l'chumra*"). We would then be compelled to follow the more severe opinions. In the case in point, the doors on the *reshus ha'rabbim* would have to be more real and functional than symbolic and ineffectual (see below, note 39).

That, however, is not all we have to know! There are several basic distinctions between true walls and *tzuros ha'pesach.* To understand these differences, let us see what the *Tur* says elsewhere:[35]

> [If an area is partially enclosed by walls] that precisely incorporate equal parts of open space [*parutz*] and built up structure [*omed* - this scenario is called: *"parutz k'omed"*], measured either vertically (fig. 2),[36] or horizontally (fig. 3),[37]

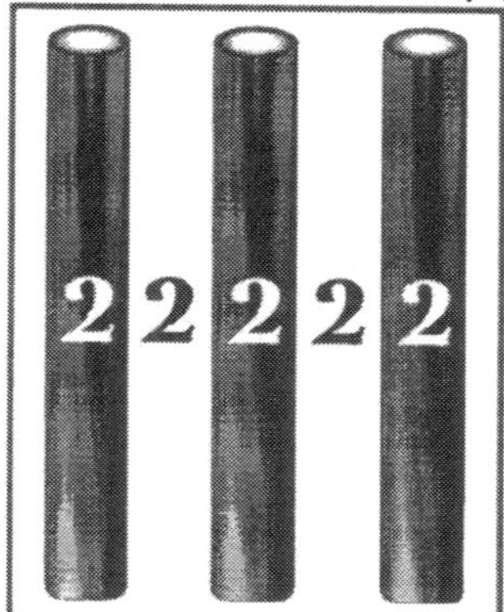

Fig. 2

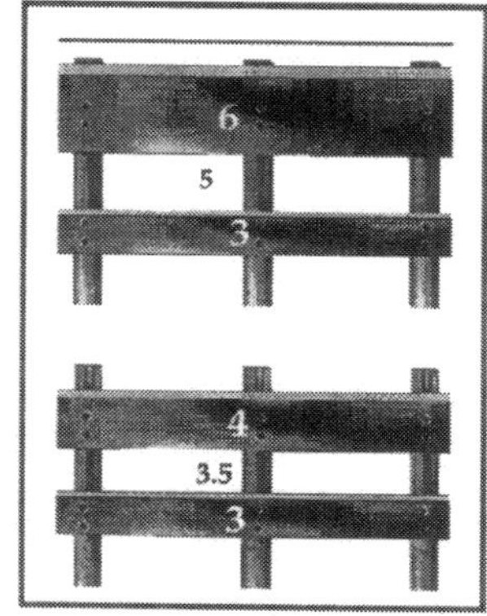

Fig. 3

> it is permissible to carry within the enclosed area - if there is no break of more than ten *amos* together in one place. Breaks of up to ten *amos* are allowed because they are regarded as openings.
>
> The presence of a doorway [*tzuras ha'pesach*] allows even breaks that are longer than ten *amos.*

---

[35] *Orach Chaim* 362-363.

[36] See the *Sha'ar Ha'Tziyun* 362:34 and the *Chazon Ish, Orach Chaim,* 68:9.

[37] The *Bi'ur Halacha* 362:9 *d.h. Ba'Erev* is perplexed as to how a horizontal *parutz k'omed* would appear. The drawing is that of the *Chazon Ish*, ibid., for omed merubeh.

According to the *Rambam* this leniency does not apply to [a scenario] where the enclosure is made up of more open space than built up structure [*parutz merubeh al ha'omed*].

The *Ri* [*Rabbeinu Yitzchok,* the *Ba'al HaTosafos*],

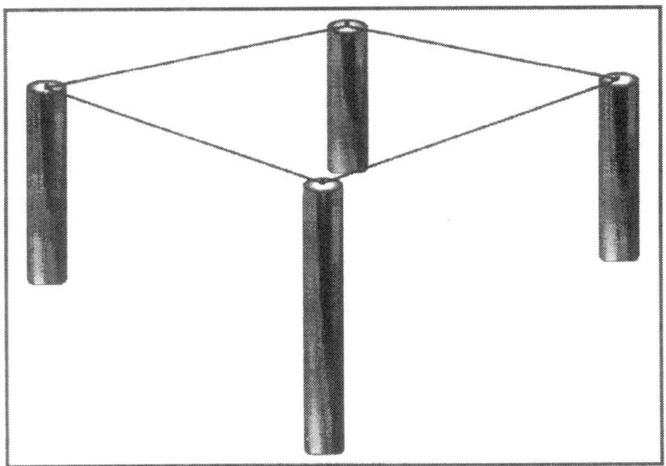

Fig. 4

however, asserts that even if an area's enclosure consists entirely of *tzuros ha'pesach* made up of four poles planted in the ground at the four corners [of the area] and a lintel atop them (fig. 4),[38] that is a sufficient enclosure. This, however, is only effective [for an *eruv*] in a courtyard [*chatzer*] or street [*mavoi*] that includes homes. *Tzuros ha'pesach* do not suffice to create enclosures for the purpose of carrying in an open field [*bik'ah*].[39] We are only subject to this restriction against

---

[38] The *Chazon Ish*, ibid., 70:23 and 111:5, writes that the "lintel" of the doorway (the "*kaneh she'al gabeihem*") should be narrower in width than the "door posts" (the "*lechayayim*") that support them. At a minimum, where a "broad" lintel is incorporated in a *tzuras ha'pesach*, the posts should be placed under the one of the edges of the lintel, so that they protrude inward or outward slightly beyond the lintel (fig. 5, see overleaf). See below, Chapter IV, note 148.

[39] The "open field" here is, of course, a *carmelis*, since if it were a *reshus ha'rabbim*, walls and doors would be necessary. See *Bi'ur Halacha* 369:10, *d.h. Aval B'Bik'ah* and the *Chazon Ish*, ibid., 70:11 who differ as to the status of a *tzuras ha'pesach eruv*

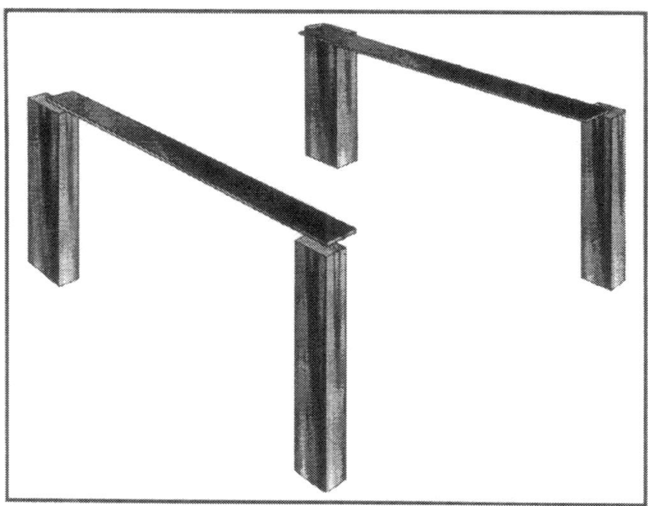

Fig. 5

the use of a *tzuras ha'pesach* as an enclosure in a *bik'ah*, however, when all four sides of the enclosed area are made up of *tzuros ha'pesach*. If, however, the enclosure is a proper one [of *parutz k'omed*], but has breaks or gaps that are longer than ten *amos*, *tzuros ha'pesach* do suffice [to close those gaps].

The Torah defines any place enclosed by three walls as an absolute *reshus ha'yachid*. The Sages, however, forbade carrying within such an area - unless some rectification is present on the fourth side as well. Since the requirement of this rectification is only rabbinic, the Sages allowed carrying

---

consisting of poles at intervals of less than ten *amos*.

In the subsequent *Bi'ur Halacha, d.h. Keshekol HaRuchos*, there is a discussion of whether a *tzuras ha'pesach* in a *reshus ha'rabbim* is at least effective enough to "downgrade" the prohibition from a *d'oraysa* (Torah level) to a *d'rabbanan* (rabbinic level). The *Bi'ur Halacha* does not come to a definitive conclusion. The *Shulchan Aruch HaRav, Orach Chaim*, 364:4 (in the parentheses); and the *Chazon Ish*, ibid., 70:13 and 74:4, tend to assume that a *tzuras ha'pesach* does effect such a downgrade. See *Nesivos Shabbos* 19:1, note 1.

within the area on the basis of even a minimal rectification.

If the area is a courtyard up to ten *amos* broad that is completely open on its fourth side, carrying within it is

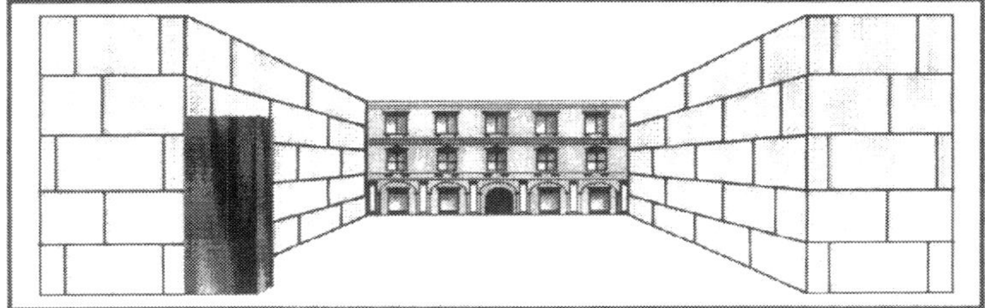

Fig. 6

permitted upon positioning a board that is four *tefachim* wide [and ten *tefachim* high] on one side of the opening (fig. 6). Alternately, if an individual finds it preferable, he may

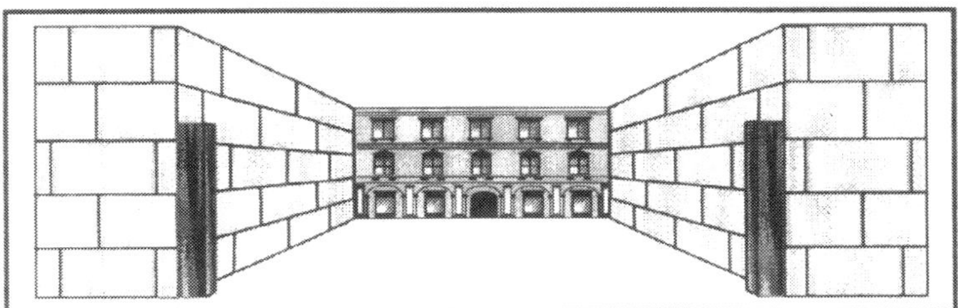

Fig. 7

employ a rectification that consists of two boards of minimal width [*"mashehu"*], one each on each side of the opening (fig. 7).[40] Since the opening takes up the entire side, even though it is less than four *tefachim* wide,[41] it requires a rectification - unless the opening is less than three *tefachim*

---

[40] See the *Mishna Berura* 363:25; and the *Chazon Ish*, ibid., 72:14, for discussions of the extent to which the two boards must be directly opposite each other.

[41] The *Mishna Berura* 363:12, notes that even if there is some actual wall on the fourth side, that will not suffice to remove the need for an additional rectification of the opening (by a beam or posts), unless there is more built up structure than open space [*omed merubeh al ha'parutz*].

wide. If the opening is more than ten *amos* wide, even if it does not take up the entire side, it must be rectified by a *tzuras ha'pesach* (fig. 8).

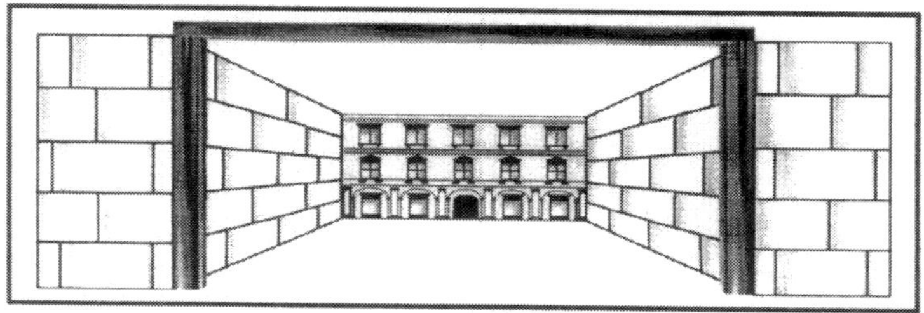

Fig. 8

The *Tur* continues to discuss the different parameters that apply to a street [*mavoi*]. The *Rama*[42] tells us, however, that because the precise parameters of halachic *mevo'os* are difficult to apply to modern street layouts, we are accustomed to implementing the somewhat more stringent parameters of courtyards [*chatzeiros*] to all contemporary streets.

4. Chapter Conclusion

The *Mishna Berura*[43] states that since several *Rishonim* follow the *Rambam's* opinion, it is, therefore preferable to adhere to his more stringent parameters, i.e., not to use a *tzuras ha'pesach* for the majority of an *eruv's* perimeter unless the poles are ten *amos* or less apart.

This rule is explained and expanded by the *Mishna Berura*:[44]

> "[Quote from the *Rama*:] All of our streets are defined as courtyards." - This is because our streets do not have houses

---

[42] *Shulchan Aruch*, ibid., 363:26.

[43] 362:59.

[44] 363:111.

[opening into] courtyards [that in turn] open into them [the streets]. They are therefore not permitted by the post or beam that normally suffices for a street.

Although a courtyard [even one that is open on both of its opposite sides] only requires two posts [one on each side of each of its openings] - not a *tzuras ha'pesach* - nevertheless, a street that is open on both of its opposite ends certainly requires the greater stringency of a *tzuras ha'pesach* (even if no homes or courtyards open into it). [This is because], generally, either: a) one of the street's ends opens into a *reshus ha'rabbim* or *carmelis*; or, b) its openings are wider than ten *amos* - in which case even a courtyard requires a *tzuras ha'pesach*, as mentioned previously in *se'if* 2.[45] That is why it is always customary to construct *tzuros ha'pesach*.

[This requirement of *tzuras ha'pesach* only applies to one of the two ends of an open-ended street.] As to the other end of the street - if it is no wider than ten *amos* - there are various opinions among the *Acharonim*. Many of them hold that it suffices to place there posts on each side of that opening, and that no *tzuras ha'pesach* is required. They reason that no matter what status we impart to this street, such a rectification suffices: If its status is that of a *mavoi* that is open at both ends, then as we learnt in *siman* 364 [*se'if* 1], it requires only a *tzuras ha'pesach* on one end and a single post or beam on the other. If, as we have previously learnt, the status [of a contemporary street] is that of a courtyard, then it needs only posts on each side of each opening [and even the *tzuras ha'pesach* on the one side would only be a stringency]. Other *Acharonim* suggest that custom dictates that *tzuros ha'pesach* be constructed at both ends. It is certainly preferable to be stringent in this regard. In

---

[45] See *Rama, Shulchan Aruch*, ibid., 363:27, that the leniency that allows a post or beam to suffice in a courtyard only applies to cases where the courtyard does not open into a *reshus ha'rabbim* but rather into another street that in turn opens into a *reshus ha'rabbim*. Thus, a courtyard that does open into a *reshus ha'rabbim* would require a *tzuras ha'pesach*. Since we treat all our streets as courtyards, they require *tzuros ha'pesach*.

troublesome cases,[46] however, such as where the overhead cable tends to break on *Shabbos* or similar situations, it appears that one can rely on the leniency [of posts at the one end where the other end has a *tzuras ha'pesach*], even if that side [with the twin posts] is open in its entirety - if that opening is less than ten *amos* long.

[46] Although the *Mishna Berura* here uses a term, *"makom ha'dechak,"* that might be taken to indicate a leniency that may be relied upon only in extreme circumstances (see below, Chapter IV, note 1), it is evident from the context here - i.e., that he advocates the stringent position on the basis of customary practice - that his terminology here does not possess the same implication as the term *"she'as ha'dechak,"* - terminology that limits leniency to cases where there are extraordinarily compelling reasons to allow an *eruv*, even though it incorporates significant leniencies - but, rather, any case where an inconvenience or practical difficulty prevents one from following the preferred practice.

Chapter II

THE MUNICIPAL ERUV: ITS HISTORY AND EVOLUTION

1. Early Positive Perspectives

We have already noted that for thousands of years the issues surrounding the construction of municipal *eruvin* were relatively minor. It was rare to find any street within a city that met even the most stringent criterion of *reshus ha'rabbim* (see below Chapter III). It is, therefore, not surprising that we find many earlier sources evincing a positive attitude toward the construction of municipal *eruvin*. Already in the times of the *Ga'onim* (the Babylonian authorities of the epoch that commenced shortly after the redaction of the Talmud, preceding the *Rishonim*), the authoritative compendium of halachic conclusions known as the *"Halachos Gedolos" ("BeHaG")* writes:[47]

> It is incumbent upon a locality to construct an *eruv* consisting of either ropes or a *tzuras ha'pesach* and enclose itself.

Several hundred years later, in the thirteenth century, the *Rosh* writes:[48]

> I have already written to you concerning the concept of an *eruv* to allow carrying in streets that are open on either end, that in all the areas where Jews live among gentiles [that

[47] Vilna edition, p. 54. We have culled much of the material cited in this Chapter from Rabbi Dov M. Kroizer's masterful essay on the issues surrounding the construction of an *eruv* in Manhattan in *Noam* vol. 1, pp. 193-233. See also the entry on *eruv* in J. D. Eisenstein's *Otzar Yisroel* encyclopedia, which includes several paragraphs on the *eruv* in Manhattan, vol. 8, pp. 138-139.

[48] *Teshuvos* [Responsa - singular: *teshuva*] *HaRosh* 21:8-9. Similar sentiments were expressed, a couple of centuries later, by the *Tashbetz* 2:37.

> *eruv*] consists of a *tzuras ha'pesach*. You forbade such [an *eruv*] for the congregation of Freres. You wrote me your proofs, and I clarified to you that they were incorrect. I warned you that you must recant and notify the congregation that they should construct [an *eruv*] for their streets. Now I have been told that you are still defiant, and thus causing the masses to desecrate the *Shabbos*. I therefore order you, upon your receipt of this letter before witnesses, to fix the streets that open into the *reshuyos ha'rabbim* in which gentiles reside with *tzuros ha'pesach*. If you do not fix the streets as I have written, I will excommunicate you. Were you to have lived at the times of the Sanhedrin they would have executed you, as you have uprooted [the principles of] the Talmud edited by Rav Ashi, and you argue on all the [Torah] giants until our times, both those who have died, may their memory be a blessing, and those who are still alive...

We note that already in these early sources, the use of an *eruv* based on *tzuras ha'pesach* was heavily promoted.[49] It seems, however, that these *eruvin* were not meant to include entire cities, but rather to enclose the streets and enclaves where Jews resided.

Later, in the last decade of the seventeenth century, we find the *Chacham Tzvi* addressing the possibility that natural walls, such as the canals surrounding The Hague in Holland,[50] or even the cliffs surrounding the entire British isle,[51] might constitute an *eruv*. While

---

[49] Historically, *Chassidim* have been more inclined to promote the construction and use of *eruvin* than *Misnagdim*. This tradition commenced with the founding of *Chassidus*, as the *Beis Aharon* - Rabbi Aharon *"HaGadol"* of Karlin (*Likutim*, p. 289) - reports that the *Ba'al Shem Tov* himself said that he came to this world to rectify three areas: to insure the proper slaughter (*shechitah*) of animals; to encourage the construction and use of *eruvin*; and, to promote more extensive use of *mikvah*. The first letters of the Hebrew terms for each of these three areas: *Zevicha, Eruvin, Mikveh*, form the acrostic: *"ZA'aM."* The *Beis Aharon* interprets the verse in *Chabakuk* 3:12: "In *ZA'aM* the land shall march," as alluding to these three rectifications, that by them the land will march toward proper underpinnings.

[50] *Chacham Tzvi, siman* 5.

[51] Ibid., *siman* 37.

he rejected the latter possibility, he did accept the former possibility, ruling:

> In this manner, if the city of The Hague, or any other city, is surrounded by a trench that is at least ten *tefachim* deep and four *tefachim* wide, it is just like a city surrounded by a high wall with doors that close, and may implement an *eruv* or *shituf* just as they can.

Other *Poskim* issued similar rulings concerning Rotterdam, Constantinople and other cities with comparable topographies.

2. *Issues Concerning Riverbank and Seashore-Based Eruvin*

The *Chacham Tzvi*'s son, Rabbi Yaakov Emden,[52] however, clarified that his father would only allow dependence on artificial trenches, not natural cliffs (as the *Chacham Tzvi* himself writes in explaining why all England is not one immense *reshus ha'yachid*). The reason for this is that natural walls are generally not valid enclosures for a *reshus ha'rabbim*, as the presence of masses within such walls, and/or their travel through or over such walls, override the walls (the concept of: *"asu rabbim u'mevatlei mechitzta,"* "the masses come and cancel the wall," which we will return to discuss in greater detail below in Sections 4 and 5; in Chapter III, Section 6; and, in Chapter IV, Section 7).[53]

These rulings were not without controversy. An issue concerning the use of lake/seashores or river/canal banks, raised by the *Rama*,[54] is that even where the shores or banks are sufficiently steep to form a halachic wall when the *eruv* is first put into effect, they may later be obliterated by a build-up of sediment. There was also concern that the river may freeze. Where, however, the wall above the highest tide is sufficient to meet the minimum standards, neither of these two

---

[52] *She'eilas Ya'avetz* 1:7.

[53] *Aruch HaShulchan, Orach Chaim* 363:48-50.

[54] *Shulchan Aruch, Orach Chaim* 363:29.

concerns would impede upon the incorporation of the banks in an *eruv*.[55]

Another problem, first addressed by the *Noda B'Yehuda*,[56] (some hundred years after the *Chacham Tzvi's teshuvos* were issued) is the possibility that bridges over the shores or banks override the walls at that point and require, across their spans, separate *tzuros ha'pesach*. Yet another concern was that the boats and ships that rode over the walls in entering and exiting port might similarly override the walls.[57]

3. *Modern Developments*

We have already mentioned that the nineteenth century brought new issues. For the first time since the destruction of Yerushalayim and the subsequent dispersion, the possibility that cities inhabited by Jews included bona fide *reshuyos ha'rabbim* became a reality.[58]

---

[55] *Mishna Berura* 363:121. The *Tikvas Zecharia* (see below, Section 4), pp. 14-22, maintains - and musters significant evidence to support his position - that the concern over build-up of sediment is only a problem when parts of the shore or bank comprising the halachic wall are at or near the water line. Where, however, the entire portion of the shore or bank comprising the halachic wall is safely above the water line, the concern is not relevant and need not be taken into account. This is the prevalent view - see *Mishna Berura*, ibid., and *Nesivos Shabbos* 15:10 and note 25. The *Mishna Berura* also notes that most sources raise the concern of sediment only when discussing seashores, not riverbanks. In discussing riverbanks, however, they are concerned only with freezing. A great river such as the Mississippi, however, may be more similar in these respects to a sea (although the *Tikvas Zecharia*, p. 56, does not entertain that possibility). (There were *Poskim* who permitted one side of an *eruv* to consist of a seashore or riverbank, if the other three were bona fide walls or *tzuros ha'pesach* - see *No'am*, ibid., pp. 214-217, and *Nesivos Shabbos*, ibid.) We should note that the *eruv* in Manhattan (see below, Section 5) did include banks and shores that were not of sufficient halachic height above the waterline, and that other rationales were necessary to allow leniency there. See *No'am*, ibid., pp. 213-217. See also *Hilchos Eruvin* by Rabbi Elimelech Lange (Yerushalayim, 1972) 3:8-12.

[56] *Noda B'Yehuda, Mahadura Tinyana, siman* 42. We will discuss this *teshuva* in greater detail in Chapter IV, note 168.

[57] See the *Aruch HaShulchan* cited in note 53 and the *Mishna Berura* cited in note 55.

[58] We will discuss this issue in detail in Chapter III.

Almost simultaneously, an abundance of *tzuros ha'pesach* suddenly materialized, in the forms of utility (telegraph, later telephone and electric) lines and raised train tracks.[59] As walls fell, attention was fixed on these structures as replacements.

The end of the nineteenth century and the beginning of the twentieth century thus brought a significant surge in halachic literature dealing with all these topics. This swell was also, largely, a result of the Jewish migration to North America. Many great cities on this continent were case studies of all the possible questions and solutions involved in the new topographies and censuses. At the same time, the socioeconomic reality - that compelled many immigrants to work on *Shabbos*; and religious milieu - the unfortunately large rise in numbers of Jews that would not refrain from carrying on *Shabbos*[60] - drove several prominent rabbinic authorities of the time to attempt the implementation of *eruvin* in their communities.

4. St. Louis

The earliest recorded attempt to organize an urban *eruv* in North America was undertaken by Rabbi Zecharia Yosef Rosenfeld, Chief Rabbi of St. Louis, Missouri, in the middle of the last decade of the nineteenth century. It seems that the *eruv* was never implemented, as Rabbi Rosenfeld died shortly after making his proposal. The initiative did result, however, in a remarkable pamphlet, *Tikvas Zecharia* ("The Hope of Zecharia"), published in St. Louis in 1896.[61] We will refer to

---

[59] We will discuss this issue in detail in Chapter IV.

[60] In the foreword to his pamphlet *Tikvas Zecharia* (see below), Rabbi Rosenfeld notes that American Jews would not hesitate to carry their *talleisim* to *Shul* on *Shabbos* (in public) without the benefit of an *eruv*. (This is, perhaps, a uniquely American phenomenon of misplaced priorities!) He goes on to say that persuasion and rebuke had proven fruitless, and that is why he then had gone on to pursue an alternate method of preventing transgression - by constructing an *eruv*. In the introduction he notes that *Chasam Sofer, Orach Chaim, siman* 99, writes that it is incumbent upon the rabbi of a city to construct an *eruv* in his locality to prevent such grave sins. He continues to amass more evidence that this is a halachic obligation.

[61] The author writes that he sent the pamphlet to Kovno, Lithuania, in an attempt to secure the *haskama* of the generation's foremost halachic authority, Rabbi Yitzchok

his positions on the definition of *reshus ha'rabbim* and the use of telegraph lines as *tzuras ha'pesach* in the Chapters devoted to those topics. Here we will address the issues presented by natural and artificial walls and barriers.

The St. Louis Jewish community of 1896 was centered in an area that is now in the downtown business district, around the intersections of Washington Ave and North Seventh to Ninth St. (the *Tikvas Zecharia* itself was printed at a press at 1024 North 7th St.). Rabbi Rosenfeld writes that this area is entirely enclosed:[62]

> On the east side by the Mississippi River.
>
> On the south side by the River Des Peres. Both rivers have banks which are more than ten *tefachim* high above their respective waterlines.
>
> On the north side by the Mississippi River as well, whose banks consist of high cliffs. Closer in to the city, however, railroads run atop artificial embankments. One embankment, that is longer than the others and steep, covers the pipelines that bring water into the city.
>
> On the west side there is a deep artificial trench that runs [south] from its northern corner where it meets the Mississippi River. Several bridges that are broader than ten *amos* traverse this trench. In that vicinity there are also walls that consist of the fences surrounding Jewish and non-Jewish cemeteries in the area, and many hills, but there are breaks broader than ten *amos* between them.
>
> On the west side there is an additional barrier [running

Elchonon Spektor. Reb Yitzchok Elchonon wrote back that he was not familiar with the reality in America, and directed Rabbi Rosenfeld to turn for a *haskama* to Rabbi Yaakov Yosef, the first (and last) Chief Rabbi of New York. Rabbi Rosenfeld's pamphlet is graced by Rabbi Yosef's approbation, as well as complimentary letters from Rabbi Shabsai Rosenberg of Brooklyn, NY; Rabbi Abba Chaim Levinson of Baltimore, MD; Rabbi Yosef Komisarsky of Chicago, IL; and, Rabbi Todros Yokel Tiktin, also of Chicago.

[62] *Tikvas Zecharia* pp. 42-43.

parallel to the network of trenches and hills mentioned previously] between the area in which the Jews reside and the areas inhabited by non-Jews. The telegraph lines begin on a hill on the north and continue right up to the walls of the River Des Peres on the south, so that there is no break either in the northwest corner or in the southwest corner between the telegraph poles and the northern and southern walls [of the *eruv*].

Rabbi Rosenfeld goes on to address the issues concerning *eruvin* based on river banks and shores. He notes the previously mentioned ruling, that riverbanks that rise to halachically sufficient heights above the highest water lines are not subject to the concerns over sediment or freezing. He rejects the lenient opinion of the great Galician *Posek* Rabbi Shlomo Kluger, that a bridge over a riverbank does not override the wall below it. Rabbi Rosenfeld negates the problem of the bridges to the west and south of St. Louis, as they all have *tzuros ha'pesach* (of telegraph lines) that cross their ramps. It is these *tzuros ha'pesach* that Rabbi Rosenfeld includes in defining the *eruv*'s perimeters, not the walls underneath.

Rabbi Rosenfeld dwells on the problem of ships and boats overriding the riverbanks. (This problem only affects natural walls. Even if massive numbers of people surmount artificial walls they remain halachically valid.[63])

[63] *Tikvas Zecharia* p. 45 ff. See *Mishna Chaim*, 363:118 and the *Sha'ar Ha'Tziyun* there note 94; and *Nesivos Shabbos* 16:14 and 25:11 and note 44. The *Sha'ar Ha'Tziyun* notes that the problem of boats and ships, raised by the *Magen Avraham*, is based on the assumption that there is a fundamental distinction between artificial walls and natural walls, and that all natural walls are invalidated wherever people pass over them. The *Ritva, Eruvin* 22b (*d.h. Deha Makif*), holds that natural walls are only of lesser stature than artificial walls when they enclose an area so broad that the walls would not be visible even if one were to enjoy an uninterrupted view of the enclosed area, viz., the mountain ranges surrounding the land of Israel. According to the *Ritva*, even natural riverbanks and seashores that enclose a smaller area are not invalidated when boats and ships dock over them. It is unclear whether the interpretation of the *Sha'ar Ha'Tziyun* in the *Ritva* is precise - see the *Mossad HaRav Kook* edition of the *Ritva* there notes 452-454 - where it is also posited that the opinion attributed to the *Ritva* is, in fact, the opinion of the *Tosafos* there *d.h. Eeleima*, the *Ramban* and others, but that the *Ritva* himself (and his *Rebbe* the *Ra'ah*) hold that even artificial walls are not valid when they enclose too broad an area. It is also noted there that the *Nishmas Adam Klal* 49 and the *Maharsham* 4:1 write that the extent of a person's

Rabbi Rosenfeld writes that the boats themselves never rode over the banks of the river. The travelers embarked and departed the major riverboats via gangplanks that were extended only when passengers are getting on or off the boats. Rabbi Rosenfeld opines that this scenario is no worse than a *reshus ha'rabbim* that is locked at night.[64] He goes on to say that the smaller ferryboats between St. Louis and East St. Louis, (which overrode piers when they docked) were not problematic, because they too stopped plying their routes at night. Furthermore, passengers embarked and disembarked the ferryboats via an artificial structure that extended into the river and had doors to close it off when unused. The existence and use of this structure protected the riverbank from being halachically overridden by the movement of the ferry riders over it.

5. *Bridges: From St. Louis to New York and Beyond*

Rabbi Rosenfeld concludes his work with a paragraph about the Eads Bridge that links St. Louis and East St. Louis, explaining why, although it was more than sixteen *amos* broad and served as a major thoroughfare, its dimensions did not render it a *reshus ha'rabbim* (see below, Chapter III, Section 2). While a bona fide *reshus ha'rabbim* would require doors, here, he states, the existing *tzuras ha'pesach* sufficed: a) because the bridge narrowed in the middle of its span to

---

unaided eyesight is sixteen *mil* (*mil* = 2000 *amos*). (Rabbi Akiva Yosef Kaplan and Rabbi Chaim Twerski both noted, however, that the curvature of the earth prevents one standing at ground level from seeing much further than six *mil*; and, therefore, that it is questionable whether the source upon which the *Nishmas Adam* bases his ruling may be applied to the Halachos of *eruvin*.) See also below, Chapter 4, note 177.

In the later controversy over the Manhattan *eruv*, Rabbi Tzvi Hirsch Eisenstadt, in his *Hatza'ah L'Tikkun Eruvin b'Manhattan*, noted that all the ships docking in the port of New York docked at artificial docks, and riding over manmade walls, which they therefore did not cancel. See *No'am*, ibid., p. 218. It seems, however, that in St. Louis (in the late nineteenth century) riverboats docked right alongside the natural banks of the Mississippi River.

64 *Tikvas Zecharia* pp. 54-55. He draws a parallel between this case and the case of drawbridges discussed in the *Sha'arei Teshuva, Orach Chaim* 363:6.

sections that were less than thirteen and a third *amos* broad;[65] and, b) because the primary mode of transportation across the bridge was by rail (see below, Chapter III, Section 5).

Bridges continued to constitute a major issue, occasionally the major issue, in many of the urban *eruvin* proposed and constructed in early twentieth century North America. The chronicles of this history are replete with controversy. No area, however, has generated as much halachic literature and debate, as the city of New York and the many *eruvin* proposed or constructed in the boroughs of Manhattan, Brooklyn, and Queens. Volumes upon volumes have been written concerning the many issues involved in these *eruvin*. Many of the issues involved are beyond the scope of this work. Some are uniquely relevant to the singular circumstances of New York. We will turn later to several points and principles involved in various New York City *eruvin*. Here we will deal with bridges. First, however, some background.

Rabbi Yehoshua Siegel, commonly known as the Sherpser Rav, first arrived in New York in 1884 and settled on the Lower East Side of Manhattan. The Sherpser Rav was the foremost rabbi of Polish origin in America at the time and, for a time, was a rival of Rabbi Yaakov Yosef, the Chief Rabbi of New York, who was of Lithuanian extraction. In 1907, the Sherpser Rav published a pamphlet, *"Eruv V'Hotza'a,"*[66] that allowed the residents of the Lower East Side to carry in the streets on *Shabbos*. While many Jews of Polish and Chassidic extraction used the Lower East Side *eruv*, those of Lithuanian descent generally did not rely on the Sherpser Rav's *heter*. Indeed, a founder of Yeshivas Rabbeinu Yitzchok Elchonon, Rabbi Yehuda David Bernstein, wrote a pamphlet, *"Hilchasa Rabasa L'Shabasa,"* disputing

---

[65] Although the minimum width of a *reshus ha'rabbim* is sixteen *amos*, it need not maintain that width over its entire length. If there are sections where it narrows somewhat, the *reshus ha'rabbim* status is not negated, as long as in those sections the street is at least thirteen and a third *amos* broad. That is why Rabbi Rosenfeld notes that in this case, the sections of the bridge narrowed to less than the absolute minimum, precluding the bridge from being categorized as a *reshus ha'rabbim* - see *Shulchan Aruch*, ibid., 345:9 and below, Chapter III, note 91 and note 133.

[66] He later expounded on the topic in his *Oznei Yehoshua*, *siman* 18.

the *heter*.[67] Nevertheless, people were still carrying on the Lower East Side as late as 1941, when Rabbi Yosef Eliyahu Henkin wrote that the rationale for leniency no longer applied.[68]

What walls did the Sherpser Rav use in formulating his *heter*? The Lower East Side was surrounded on three sides by the walls that front on the East River, and on the fourth side by the Third Avenue elevated train line (fig. 9). The Brooklyn, Manhattan and Williamsburg Bridges,

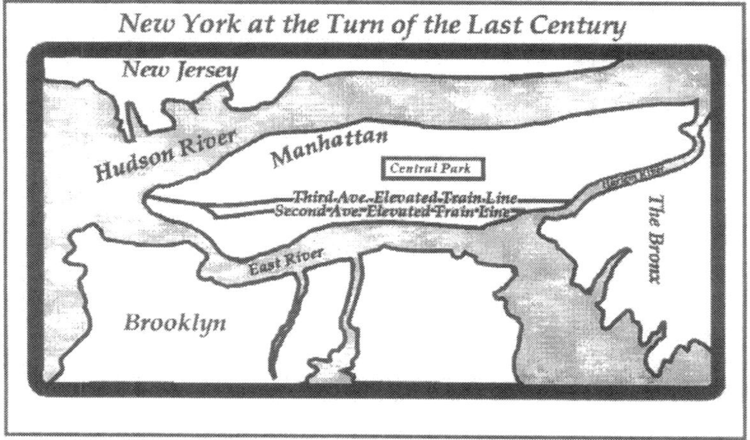

Fig. 9

however, all cross from the Lower East Side into Brooklyn, and are certainly sixteen *amos* broad. They can carry enough people to

[67] Rabbi Bernstein's primary objection was based on the assumption that many of the streets within the Lower East Side *eruv* could be considered *platyos* - see below, Chapter III, note 133, where we discuss the concept of a *platya* in some detail. See *No'am*, ibid., pp. 210-211 for the counter arguments, i.e., perhaps this was once true, but currently, however, most of the areas that might once have been deemed *platyos* are now enclosed - in large stores, convention centers and shopping malls.

[68] *Eidus L'Yisroel*, p.151. See Rabbi Gedalya Felder's *Yesodei Yeshurun - Ma'areches Lamed Tes Melachos* (Yerushalayim, 1976), pp. 276-278, for a brief overview of the history of *eruvin* in Manhattan in which many relevant sources are cited. The most exhaustive treatment of the subject is in Rabbi Menachem M. Kasher's *Divrei Menachem, Orach Chaim* vol. 2.

constitute *reshuyos ha'rabbim* (see below, Chapter III, Sections 2-3). The Sherpser Rav asserted that they, nevertheless, did not disrupt the *eruv* because they are not *"mefulash."* (This is a difficult word to translate - and that, in and of itself, has caused much halachic controversy. The word translates roughly as: directly open and through.) The bridges do not lead to or from streets that cut directly across Manhattan and continue to bridges on the other side. The Sherpser Rav, therefore, held that they were subject only to the requirement that applies to any other opening in a wall that is more than ten *amos* broad (see below, Chapter IV, Section 6), i.e., a *tzuras ha'pesach*.[69]

This condition of *reshus ha'rabbim* is noted in several *Rishonim* and quoted in *Shulchan Aruch*.[70] Some *Rishonim*, however, do not consider *mefulash* a necessary condition of a *reshus ha'rabbim*.[71] This

---

[69] As we noted in Section 2, it is generally accepted that walls underneath a bridge - even artificial walls - are not meaningful vis-á-vis the bridge itself, and that whatever rectification is ultimately required must be mounted above and across the bridge's roadway. The nature of that rectification is contingent on whether the bridge is or serves an area classified as a *reshus ha'rabbim* (in which case *delasos* are required) or a *carmelis* (in which case a *tzuras ha'pesach* is required). See the discussion in this regard in the *Chazon*, ibid., *siman* 108, who resoundingly rejects the lenient position of the Bilsker Rav, Rabbi Ben Zion Sternfeld, in *Sha'arei Tziyon siman* 4; *Igros Moshe, Orach Chaim*, 1:139:1; and, *No'am*, ibid., pp. 224-228. See the discussions in *No'am* there as to: a) whether extant structures on the bridges may be considered halachically valid *tzuros ha'pesach*; and, b) whether drawbridges require an additional rectification. Subsequently (pp. 229-230) Rabbi Kroizer also discusses the related issue of the twenty tunnels under the various bodies of water around Manhattan.

[70] *Rashi, Eruvin* 6a, *d.h. Reshus Ha'rabbim*, and 6b, *d.h. Yerushalayim* (we will quote the former *Rashi* in full in Chapter III, Section 2); several other *Rishonim*, cited by Rabbi Kasher in *Torah Sheleima*, vol. 15 p. 177, and summarized in *No'am*, ibid., pp. 204-206; the *Tur* cited above in the introduction; the *Shulchan Aruch*, ibid., 345:7. The *Beis Ephraim* (45c in the pagination of the standard edition) we will cite in Chapter III, Section 3, that serves as the basis for all modern metropolitan *eruvin* notes that although many large cities already had populations of 600,000 people, and major thoroughfares that might meet the criteria he had listed for a *reshus ha'rabbim*, *eruvin* could still be constructed in them because the streets in urban areas rarely run straight from gate to gate. This is similar to the comment later made by Rabbi Shlomo Dovid Kahane, see below Chapter III, Section 5.

[71] *Ritva, Shabbos* 6a, *d.h. Eizehu Reshus Ha'rabbim*.

was one of the sources of contention in the Lower East Side *eruv*. When, almost a half century later, in 1949, the Amshinover *Rebbe* proposed an *eruv* that would encompass the entire island of Manhattan, the issue of the eighteen bridges around Manhattan became the major halachic issue. In his 1952 *teshuva* concerning Manhattan to Rabbi Tzvi Hirsch Eisenstadt;[72] and, in a 1981 *teshuva* concerning Brooklyn,[73] Rabbi Moshe Feinstein casts doubt on this

---

[72] *Igros Moshe*, ibid., 1:140. The only *Rishon* that Reb Moshe concedes as unambiguously requiring *mefulash* in the sense of completely straight is the *Or Zaru'a HaGadol, Eruvin, siman* 164, cited in *No'am*, ibid., p. 206. The *Or Zaru'a* states explicitly that the gates by which the *reshus ha'rabbim* traverses the city must be directly opposite each other (*"mechuvan me'sha'ar l'sha'ar"*). Reb Moshe in that *teshuva* and the previous one notes a possible dichotomy between a walled city, in which *mechuvan me'sha'ar l'sha'ar* is essential, and a non-walled city, in which only *mefulash* is necessary. See also Rabbi Elimelech Lange's *Hilchos Eruvin* (Tel Aviv, 1972), addendum to the first chapter, *se'if* 2, who makes a similar distinction.

As we will see later (Chapter III, note 33), the major proponent of the Manhattan *eruv*, Rabbi Menachem M. Kasher, held that as far as the tally of 600,000 was concerned, it was likely that Manhattan was indeed a *reshus ha'rabbim*. He therefore based his advocacy on other principles, including the prerequisite of *mefulash*. Following Rabbi Kroizer's essay, in *No'am*, ibid., pp. 233-237, Rabbi Kasher published a *teshuva* in which he musters evidence to prove that, in fact, many *Rishonim* did hold of the prerequisite of *mefulash*. It is evident from Reb Moshe's 1981 *teshuva* that he did not accept those arguments.

It is interesting that one of the difficulties that led Reb Moshe to regard the prerequisite of *mefulash* with suspicion was the question of the source for such a condition. The parameters of *reshus ha'rabbim* are derived from the manner in which the Levites travelled with the components of the *Mishkan* (the Tabernacle) in the desert after the Exodus. How can we deduce that the paths on which they traveled ran due straight?

Rabbi Kasher (ibid.) accepts this question as valid. He replies that, on the basis of several sources (see, for example, *Rashi, Eruvin*, 22b, *d.h. Ma'alos U'Morados*), it seems that *Hashem*, via the *ananei hakavod* (the clouds of glory), flattened the hills and also straightened the paths before the travelling camp.

We should note that Rabbi Eisenstadt, who toiled mightily to research and promote the Manhattan *eruv*, although not well known, was an outstanding *talmid chochom*, and is addressed by Reb Moshe in this *teshuva* and the preceding one with great respect.

[73] *Igros Moshe*, ibid., 5:28:6-7. When using this, most recent, volume of the *Igros Moshe*, it is important to be aware that some text is actually not from Reb Moshe's pen, but inserted by the editors. These insertions are recognizable by a slightly

entire concept. Reb Moshe opines that many of the *Rishonim* that mention *mefulash* as a condition of *reshus ha'rabbim* meant only that there must exist an uninterrupted thoroughfare from gate to gate - but not that this thoroughfare need run straight.[74] He goes on to say that, in any event, the requirement of *mefulash* only applies to a walled city. Reb Moshe maintains that if a city is: a) not walled; and, b) meets the 600,000 criterion (that we will discuss in Chapter III), then any sixteen *amos* wide street - or bridge - that provides access to and from the city (or an area therein) is a *reshus ha'rabbim* and can only be permitted with bona fide doors.[75]

6. Chapter Conclusion

Poskim of great stature disagreed with Reb Moshe, and Reb Moshe himself writes, in a 1961 *teshuva*, that he, therefore, did not protest against the *Rabbanim* that approved of the Manhattan *eruv*. (When *eruvin* were constructed in Brooklyn, however - in Flatbush and Boro Park - Reb Moshe wrote that there was no legitimate halachic basis for leniency. His opposition was based on his position that we will discuss below, in Chapter III, Sections 3-5. He, therefore, publicly protested against those who allowed those *eruvin*.[76]) Nevertheless,

---

smaller typeface.

[74] Thus, to use an example cited by Rabbi Kroizer, in uptown Manhattan the Washington Bridge from the Bronx to Manhattan crosses the East River at 181st St. The George Washington Bridge from Manhattan to New Jersey crosses the Hudson River at 178th St. While there is no street that runs straight across Manhattan linking the two bridges, traffic does proceed uninterrupted from bridge to bridge. That suffices to meet the criterion of *mefulash* according to Reb Moshe. According to the other *Poskim*, it does not.

[75] In *Igros Moshe*, ibid., 1:139:4, Reb Moshe rules that even if the bridges are not themselves *reshuyos ha'rabbim*, they may still generate a requirement for *delasos* if they: a) originate in areas that may be *reshuyos ha'rabbim*; and, b) provide the masses with access to those areas. The precise definition of "masses" in this context is an old, unresolved issue - see the *Bi'ur Halacha* 363:36, *d.h. Havei KeMechitza*, and *No'am*, ibid., pp. 223-224.

[76] *Igros Moshe*, ibid., 4:89 and the addendum there p. 428.

Reb Moshe's preeminent status as a *Posek HaDor* (one of the greatest halachic decisors of his generation) insured that relatively few individuals used the Manhattan *eruv*.

Chapter III

THE RESHUS HA'RABBIM ISSUE

1. The Four Domains: A Review[77]

Large cities in Israel have been halachically enclosed by *eruvin* for many decades. Little controversy is associated with these *eruvin*. Members of communities across the spectrum of observant society rely on these *eruvin* to carry objects in public on *Shabbos*. In North America, however, the widespread construction of *eruvin* in large cities is a relatively recent phenomenon. In contrast to the situation in Israel, as we have already noted, controversy and acrimony have frequently attended the process of building eruvin on this continent. Let us explore the major halachic underpinning of this distinction: the definition of *reshus ha'rabbim*.

As we have already learnt, *Chazal* identify four categories of *reshuyos* (domains) which relate to the prohibition of carrying on *Shabbos* (and, to a certain extent, *Yom Tov*). Three of these domains are *d'oraysa* in origin. *Chazal* subsequently divided one of these domains into two categories. The three domains *d'oraysa* are: private (*reshus ha'yachid*), public (*reshus ha'rabbim*), and neutral (*makom patur*). *Chazal* divided the domain of *makom patur* in two: exempt (still known as *makom patur*) and neutral (*carmelis*). Certain leniencies apply to a *makom patur*.[78] Since, however, a *makom patur d'rabbanan* is by definition an area smaller than four *tefachim* square, these leniencies are not relevant to our discussion of a community *eruv* encompassing larger areas.

The Torah only forbade carrying objects in and into a *reshus*

[77] The next few pargraphs summarize material we have already seen at greater length in Chapter I. Here we will just review the most essential parameters.

[78] We discussed them in Chapter I, Section 2. See also Rabbi Shimon Eider's *Halachos of the Eruv* (Lakewood, 1968) Chap. 1, A:4.

ha'rabbim. Carrying objects within and between a *reshus ha'yachid* or *reshus ha'rabbim* and a *carmelis* was permitted *me'd'oraysa*. *Chazal* banned carrying in and into a *carmelis* as well. *Chazal* also limited the definition of *reshus ha'yachid*. According to most *Rishonim*, an area surrounded by walls on three of its four sides is a *reshus ha'yachid d'oraysa*. *Chazal* mandated some form of enclosure on the fourth side as well.

Halacha distinguishes between the enclosure necessary to convert a *carmelis* into a *reshus ha'yachid* and the enclosure necessary to convert a *reshus ha'rabbim* into a *reshus ha'yachid*. The *Gemara*[79] relates that Yerushalayim would have been considered a *reshus ha'rabbim* had its doors not been closed at night.[80] The *Poskim* disagree over whether these doors had to have been closed *me'd'oraysa* or *me'd'rabbanan*.[81] Some sources maintain that *me'd'oraysa* a *tzuras ha'pesach* would have sufficed.[82] Others maintain that in *reshus ha'rabbim delasos* are required *me'd'oraysa*.[83]

This requirement is limited, in any event, to *reshus ha'rabbim*. An enclosure intended to surround an area that falls into the category of

---

[79] *Eruvin* 6b.

[80] According to most *Poskim*, a *reshus ha'rabbim* must be enclosed by *delasos* (doors) because otherwise, *asu rabbim u'mivatlei mechitzta* - the passage of the masses through the wall (were it to be just a *tzuras ha'pesach*) would render it invalid. We will discuss this concept in Section 6 below. The question is whether this concept negates a wall on a *d'oraysa* or *d'rabbanan* level. See also Rabbi Chaim Gedalya Tzimbalist's *Avodas Avoda* (Tel Aviv, 1973 - this work is outstanding in its explanation of the various approaches in *Messeches Eruvin* -) on the *Avodas HaKodesh* 3:1, note 2 and *Tosefes Biur siman* 1.

[81] See *Nesivos Shabbos* 23:1, note 2.

[82] We must note that this is not the only source in the *Gemara* for the requirement of doors for a *reshus ha'rabbim*. We will learn of *Poskim* who hold that even had it not had doors, Yerushalayim would not necessarily have been a *reshus ha'rabbim*. Even these *Poskim*, however, derive from other sources that a *reshus ha'rabbim d'oraysa* requires *delasos*. See *Nesivos Shabbos*, ibid., note 1.

[83] We shall return to this issue in Section 6 below.

carmelis does not require doors to allow carrying therein. The rectification of *tzuras ha'pesach* is sufficient in such cases. Clearly, therefore, it is highly advantageous to have an area defined halachically as a *carmelis* as opposed to a *reshus ha'rabbim*. Besides the lesser expense involved in building a *tzuras ha'pesach* as opposed to doors, another issue we may thus avoid is the problem involved in the use of doors that cannot be closed at night. Such doors are not completely comparable to the doors of Yerushalayim - which were closed at night. Thus, physically or legally eliminating true *reshuyos ha'rabbim* from an *eruv* averts the complex halachic problem of the extent to which the doors must be suitable for closing.[84]

Let us now explore the various definitions of *reshus ha'rabbim*.

2. *Defining Reshus Ha'Rabbim*

The most stringent definition of *reshus ha'rabbim* - and that which is most loyal to the text of the Talmud - is recorded by the *Rambam*:[85]

> Which [domains] are [categorized as] *reshus ha'rabbim*? a) Deserts; b) forests; c) marketplaces; and, d) any road that opens into them - if the road is sixteen *amos* [86] wide and is not roofed over.

Those *Poskim* that accept the *Rambam*'s opinion do not allow the construction of a *tzuras ha'pesach*-based *eruv* in any modern city. Most, if not all, contemporary urban *eruvin* include many streets that are sixteen *amos* broad (we include sidewalks in the measurement - they, too, serve as "roads" - for pedestrian traffic).

Other *Rishonim*, however, disagree with the *Rambam*. *Rashi* [87]

---

[84] See *Nesivos Shabbos*, ibid., notes 9-10.

[85] *Yad HaChazaka, Hilchos Shabbos* 14:1.

[86] See Chapter I, note 8, where we cited the two major schools of thought on the measurment of an *amah*.

[87] *Eruvin* 6a, *d. h. R"H* [*reshus ha'rabbim*].

states that a *reshus ha'rabbim* is:

> ...Sixteen *amos* broad. And a city in which there are 600,000 people that has no wall, or whose main thoroughfare runs straight ["*mefulash*"] from gate to gate - that is thus "open" just as [the expanse was "open" before the travelling camp] in the travels of the tribes in the desert [- is *reshus ha'rabbim*].

The *Tosafos*[88] note that the *Ba'al Halachos Gedolos* ("*BeHaG*") concurs with this view, and also requires this additional criterion - the presence of 600,000 people - to establish that an area is a *reshus ha'rabbim*.

The *Acharonim* tabulate the numbers of *Rishonim* on both sides of this issue.[89] These numbers run, quite literally, into the dozens. Obviously, no definitive, final, firm ruling can ever be attained in a halachic battle royal of such proportions and weight. In practice, most *Poskim* have relied on the opinion that we should classify an area as a *reshus ha'rabbim* only when the criterion of 600,000 people is met. The *Mishna Berura* says that although a *Ba'al Nefesh* (generally understood to mean one who is consistently scrupulous in fulfilling *mitzvos* in the most fastidious manner) should personally conduct himself according to the more stringent view, he may not protest against those who rely on the more lenient opinion.[90]

---

[88] Ibid., *d.h. keizad me'arvin*.

[89] See *Shemiras Shabbos K'Hilchasa* 17:3 note 21.

[90] *Orach Chaim* 345:23. Some rabbinic authorities hold that the *Mishna Berura*'s advice that a *Ba'al Nefesh* adopt the stringent position only applies to scenarios where the sole basis for leniency is that the criterion of 600,000 is not met. Where, however, other mitigating factors (viz., that the *reshuyos ha'rabbim* are not *mefulash* - according to the *Poskim* who hold of that criterion - see above, Chapter II, Section 5; that the city is walled by *omed merubeh al ha'parutz* walls; etc.) are involved, then perhaps even a *Ba'al Nefesh* might be permitted to carry.

In this vein, when first asked by the Sherpser Rav for an approbation for the Lower East Side of New York City *eruv*, the *Maharsham* responded that those who conducted themselves leniently had a sufficient basis in Halacha, but that a *Ba'al Nefesh* should conduct himself stringently. Later, however, when the Sherpser Rav

(*Rashi*'s definition contains another parameter not explicitly mentioned by the *Rambam*: *"Mefulash"* - that the thoroughfare must run straight from gate to gate. We have discussed this parameter already in Chapter II, Section 5.)

3. Space and Time Factors: Space Frame of Measurement

We must now define in what space and time the 600,000 people must be present and counted to meet the criterion for *reshus ha'rabbim*. If, for example, the space in which we count people would be all the areas included within the boundaries of a state or province, and the time over which we count the people therein would be a month, then, of course, practically every place in the world would be *reshus ha'rabbim*. If, on the other hand, the space in which we count people would be a single city block, and the time over which we count the people therein would be a minute, then, of course, practically no place in the world would be a *reshus ha'rabbim*.

These factors are matters of great contention among the *Poskim*. The definition given by *Rashi* previously in the passage that we quoted above seems to suggest that the space frame of measurement is the entire city. *Rashi* also seems to hold that there is no time frame of measurement. Thus, a literal interpretation of *Rashi*'s position would lead us to the conclusion that any city that contains 600,000

---

wrote to him more extensively on the topic, the *Maharsham* reversed his earlier position and stated that even a *Ba'al Nefesh* could conduct himself leniently - see Rabbi Kroizer's essay in *No'am*, vol. 1, p. 193, ff., and *Yesodei Yeshurun, Ma'areches Lamed Tes Melachos*, part 2, p. 277. To assume that the *Mishna Berura* would also be inclined to allow a *Ba'al Nefesh* to conduct himself leniently when additional mitigating factors are involved in a modern metropolitan *eruv* seems, nevertheless, speculative.

We should also note that the rationale underlying a prevalent "gender dichotomy" in the use of *eruvin* between husbands that do not use an *eruv* while their wives do so, is based on the *Mishna Berura*'s assertion that a *Ba'al Nefesh* should conduct himself stringently. The line of reasoning is that: a) baseline "Halacha" permits the use of *eruvin*; b) it is a stringency [*"chumra"*] not to use *eruvin*; therefore, c) it is legitimate for one or more members of a family to adopt the stringent position while others observe the "baseline" Halacha.

people (most likely including both residents and commuters), is a *reshus ha'rabbim* in its entirety. Some *Poskim* rule accordingly.[91]

Others propose alternate interpretations of *Rashi's* meaning. Rabbi Moshe Feinstein[92] interprets *Rashi's* opinion on the basis of a *Tosafos*

---

[91] I have heard the stringent view expressed in the name of Rabbi Aharon Soloveichik.

In the *Bigdei Shesh* on *Bava Basra* p. 310, note 71a, based on the *Rashbam* in *Bava Basra* 60a and the words of *Rashi* himself in *Shabbos* 96b *d.h. Machane Levi'ah*, this author presents an alternate interpretation of *Rashi*'s definition. I subsequently saw that the *Tikvas Zecharia*, p. 9, offers the same interpretation, i.e., that when the Jews were in the desert after leaving Egypt, it was actually only the *Machane Levi'ah*, the area where the Levites were camped, that was a true *reshus ha'rabbim*, because it was there that the 600,000 men between the ages of 20 and 60 gathered to receive the word of G-d from Moshe *Rabbeinu*. The other sectors of the Israelite encampment were open to the *Machane Levi'ah*, and all the pathways that led there were, therefore, extensions of that *reshus ha'rabbim*. Thus, in order for a city that has 600,000 inhabitants to be considered *reshus ha'rabbim*, it must contain a central area or street where those inhabitants are accustomed to gathering. It is only then that all the other streets that lead to that one central plaza or thoroughfare may also be considered *reshuyos ha'rabbim*.

In his analysis of the definition of *reshus ha'rabbim*, the *Aruch HaShulchan, Orach Chaim* 345:14-22 takes this concept to a further extreme, and states that there are essentially no *reshuyos ha'rabbim* in our times. He opines that an essential component of the definition of *reshus ha'rabbim* is that it serve as the central thoroughfare (*sratya*) or plaza (*platya*), for the entire city. Since none of our cities have one central thoroughfare that constitutes the main access route to and from the city, nor do they have one central plaza that serves to amass the population of the city - à la the *Machane Levi'ah* in the desert - there are no longer any true *reshuyos ha'rabbim* in our midst. Many *Poskim* will only use the *Aruch HaShulchan*'s opinion as an additional reason to be inclined toward leniency (a "*snif*") when there are other mitigating factors. See *Igros Moshe, Orach Chaim*, 5:28:9 and *Nesivos Shabbos* 3:1, note 9.

(We should note that, according to both the position advocated by Rabbi Soloveichik here, and that advanced by Rabbi Feinstein cited below, <u>all</u> the streets in certain areas can be considered *reshus ha'rabbim*. Other opinions differentiate between streets that run perpendicular to a *reshus ha'rabbim* and streets that continue in the same direction where a *reshus ha'rabbim* ends. The latter are generally considered *reshuyos ha'rabbim* - even if they are not sixteen *amos* wide and do not sustain the traffic necessary to constitute a *reshus ha'rabbim* in and of themselves. See *Shulchan Aruch, Orach Chaim* 345:8-9 and 364:1; above, Chapter I, note 65; and, below, Section 5.)

[92] *Igros Moshe, Orach Chaim* 1:139.5. See, however, *Aruch HaShulchan*, ibid., 345:26, and above, note 91.

that discusses the parameters of *reshus ha'rabbim*. The *Tosafos* state:[93]

> ...All of our *reshuyos ha'rabbim* are in fact *carmelis*, because our streets are not sixteen *amos* wide, nor do 600,000 people travel in it...

Reb Moshe notes the discrepancy between the plural tense at the beginning of the statement and the single tense at the end of the statement. Reb Moshe resolves the apparent contradiction with an original approach: In a city that contains a total of 600,000 people, every street is considered a *reshus ha'rabbim*. Reb Moshe interprets the previously mentioned *Rashi* in a similar vein: A city through which 600,000 people travel is a *reshus ha'rabbim*. Therefore, any street in that city - that is at least sixteen *amos* wide - is a *reshus ha'rabbim* (and can only be halachically rectified with doors).

This approach is significantly more lenient than the first approach that we examined. The former approach views any city in which 600,000 residents and/or commuters are present as a *reshus ha'rabbim*. The latter approach requires that the 600,000 people must be present in the streets to make up a *reshus ha'rabbim*. People who remain inside their homes are not included in the halachic tally.[94]

In later *teshuvos* Reb Moshe clarifies his approach further.[95] He estimates that, to assume that 600,000 people frequent the streets of a city, the city must be inhabited by four to five times that amount of people. He further refines his approach by stating two limitations: a)

---

[93] *Shabbos* 64b, *d.h. Rabbi Anani*.

[94] Reb Moshe uses his approach to resolve a major difficulty for the school of thought that requires 600,000 people to constitute a *reshus ha'rabbim*, raised by the *Tosafos, Shabbos* 6a, *d.h. Keitzad Me'arvin*: Since the number of actual people (including women, children, the elderly, and the accompanying *erev rav* - non-Jews who converted and were thus not affiliated with any of the enumerated tribes) in the desert far exceeded 600,000, why is this the number associated with the definition of *reshus ha'rabbim*? The *Tosafos* themselves answer that we can only use the number explicit in the Torah. See below, Section 5, for Reb Moshe's explanation and further discussion.

[95] *Igros Moshe*, ibid., 4:87-89. Additional material relevant to *siman* 89 is included in an addendum in that volume, p. 428.

areas included in municipal boundaries but separated by geographical barriers (viz., Manhattan, which is separated from Brooklyn by a river) are not to be combined in the halachic tally; and, b) a city whose municipal boundaries are very broad is not measured as one unit. Each twelve *mil* by twelve *mil* block (approximately eight miles by eight miles) is measured separately.[96] The rationale underlying this ruling is that the encampment of the Jews in the desert - from which the Halachos of *hotza'a* and *reshuyos* are derived - was of such dimensions. These, therefore, are the defining dimensions of *reshus ha'rabbim*.

Reb Moshe also qualifies that distinct neighborhoods and suburbs may be considered separate from adjacent large cities and larger twelve *mil* by twelve *mil* blocks. In a 1974 *teshuva*,[97] he writes that the neighborhood of Kew Garden Hills in the borough of Queens, New York City, is a "small city," and, therefore, that an *eruv* in that community alone would not be subject to the position that he shared with Rabbi Aharon Kotler against the construction of *eruvin* in large cities.[98] In his first (1978) *teshuva* to the *Va'ad HaRabbonim* of Flatbush, Reb Moshe writes that all of Brooklyn is to be regarded as one large city, and that the neighborhoods within the borough cannot be regarded as distinct entities.[99] In a 1980 *teshuva*, Reb Moshe writes

---

[96] One *mil* = 2000 *amos*. See above, Chapter 1, note 8. These blocks must be drawn in the most stringent manner possible. In other words, if we need to know if a certain area is a *reshus ha'rabbim*, we need to extend these imaginary blocks in all the possible manners and directions. Municipal boundaries do not limit these blocks. A block drawn in Tel Aviv, for instance, would extend into Bnei Brak and Petach Tikva, even though the latter are distinct municipalities. This principle holds true even according to the most lenient approach - that we will see below - that we measure each street independently: A street that traverses several towns is still regarded as one street in the halachic tally. See *Techumin* vol. 10, p. 139.

[97] *Igros Moshe*, ibid., 4:86.

[98] See the Introduction, note 5.

[99] *Igros Moshe*, ibid., 4:87. In several places, however, Reb Moshe writes that the Brooklyn neighborhood of Seagate is distinct from the rest of the borough, because of its unique situation of being bounded by the ocean on three sides and a fence on the fourth side. See *Igros Moshe*, ibid., 5:28:19 where he summarizes his previous *teshuvos* on the topic.

that Oak Park and Southfield, suburbs that are adjacent to Detroit, are distinct from the large city that they adjoin.[100] The following year, in a detailed *teshuva* concerning the Flatbush and Boro Park *eruvin*, he writes that while there was a large municipal *eruv* in Warsaw which had a population of more than 600,000, nevertheless, there were never 600,000 people in the streets, as this would require close to 3,000,000 inhabitants, and Warsaw was not even half as large.[101] In other Eastern European cities, Reb Moshe continues, the *eruvin* were only in the small neighborhoods in which the Jews lived, not in large areas such as Flatbush and Boro Park that do meet the requirements for 600,000. (In this, final *teshuva* on the topic, he notes that each of these neighborhoods unto themselves may fulfill the requirements for 600,000.)

Rabbi Chaim Ozer Grodziensky seems to maintain a similar definition.[102] In a 1938 *teshuva* to Paris, he contends that were it not surrounded by walls, Paris would be considered a *reshus ha'rabbim*, because 600,000 people travel throughout the city. He specifically notes that it is not necessary to identify specific streets that service 600,000 people. Unlike Reb Moshe, however, Reb Chaim Ozer does not attempt to define more specific parameters, as a clarification of how to assess the census is not the basis of his lenient ruling in the *teshuva*.

The most lenient approach is that found in the text of the *Shulchan Aruch*:[103]

> Some say that any [street] which 600,000 people do not traverse every day is not a *reshus ha'rabbim*.

---

100 *Igros Moshe*, ibid., 5:29.

101 *Igros Moshe*, ibid., 5:28:5. Since Reb Moshe was not precise in delineating the principles of when we regard neighborhhods as part of a larger city and when we regard them as distinct from it, an issue that has frequently been the subject of debate in subsequent urban *eruvin* is how Reb Moshe would have regarded them.

102 *Achi'ezer* 4:8. This *teshuva* is printed in the new (1987) editions of the *Achi'ezer*.

103 *Orach Chaim* 345:7.

This is obviously a very lenient definition. The *Mishna Berura* writes:[104]

> I searched through all the *Rishonim* who maintain this opinion [that the presence of 600,000 people is necessary to establish a *reshus ha'rabbim*] and did not find this criterion [that the people pass through every day] mentioned in their writings, rather only a criterion that 600,000 people can be found [occasionally] in that place.

Although the *Mishna Berura* echoes the sentiment of many *Poskim*, the *Shulchan Aruch*'s ruling is grounded in legitimate sources.[105] Other *Poskim* offer their own interpretations of the manner in which we count the 600,000 people.

It seems that the generally accepted approach is that of the *Beis Ephraim*.[106] The *Beis Ephraim* and the *Mishkenos Ya'akov*[107] argued the case of *eruvin* in modern metropolitan areas. Their *teshuvos* provide the main resource of material both lenient (*Beis Ephraim*) and stringent (*Mishkenos Ya'akov*) on this subject. Rabbi Elimelech Lange summarizes the approach of the *Beis Ephraim*:[108]

---

104 345:24.

105 See the *Chiddushei HaRamban* on *Shabbos* 57a, end of *d.h. Masnisin Lo B'Chutei Tzemer* and *Rabbeinu Nissim* on the *Rif, Shabbos* 26a (in the pagination of the *Rif*), *d.h. Aval Kashe* who hold like the *Shulchan Aruch*. See also *Nesivos Shabbos* 3:1, note 9; and *Hilchos Eruvin*, Appendix to Chap. 1, Chapter 4. An exhaustive assessment and tabulation of the statements found in the works of the *Rishonim* that support the *Shulchan Aruch*'s ruling was published by Rabbi Menachem M. Kasher in *Torah Sheleimah*, vol. 15, beginning on page 172. A synopsis of his conclusions can be found in Rabbi Dov M. Kroizer's essay in *No'am*, vol. 1, pp. 202-203.

106 Rabbi Ephraim Zalman Margolios, Rabbi of Brody, Poland, (d. 1828). *Orach Chaim* 26 (p. 46a).

107 Rabbi Yaakov Schick, Rabbi of Karlin, Lithuania (one of the greatest students of Rabbi Chaim of Volozhin, d. 1845). *Orach Chaim* 109-111 (in some editions 120-122).

108 *Hilchos Eruvin* ibid.

The criterion of 600,000 consists of three [conditions]: a) *"Metzuyim"* - that 600,000 people should be present in the area; b) *"Bok'im"* - that they should frequently travel along the specific street in question; c) *"Bechol yom"* - that it be possible that they might all travel on that street in one day. This is the language of the *Beis Ephraim* in his *teshuva:* "According to *Rashi* it is necessary that a road possess the capacity to bear the traffic of the 600,000 people present in its environs, so that it would be possible that all those people might pass through that street in one day."

4. Space and Time Factors: Time, and Practical Differences

By now it should be evident that the *Poskim* are not in agreement on the period over which we count the 600,000 people. It seems from Reb Moshe's earlier *teshuvos* that his opinion is that we tally the 600,000 from a "freeze-frame" perspective. This would mean that if there was any moment at which 600,000 people were out in the streets of the area in question it would be a *reshus ha'rabbim.* It is clear, however, from Reb Moshe's later *teshuvos* that this is not accurate.[109] In fact, Reb Moshe maintains that to define an area as a *reshus ha'rabbim* there must be (at least some) days during the year during which "throughout the time that people normally leave their houses" there are 600,000 people in - all the streets together - every moment of the day.

According to the *Beis Ephraim,* however, we establish the tally over the course of an entire day, i.e., if the sum of travelers on the street over the course of an entire day adds up to 600,000, the street qualifies as a *reshus ha'rabbim.*[110]

---

109 I am indebted to Rabbi Chaim Twerski for correcting my original impression from *Igros Moshe,* ibid., 4:87-88. The quotation in text here is from *siman* 87.

110 We must note and disclaim: By presenting here only a few specific *Poskim* we are certainly guilty of oversimplification. In reality, of course, many, many more *Poskim* have issued opinions on these issues. We have limited our discussion to a few salient examples in the hope of avoiding confusion and achieving clarity. Those interested in further breadth and depth will find more material in the sources cited in the notes.

A noteworthy distinction between these two approaches pertains to the question of which streets become *reshuyos ha'rabbim* when the relevant conditions exist. According to Reb Moshe, every street in an area in which we find 600,000 people in all the streets together becomes a *reshus ha'rabbim*. According to the *Beis Ephraim*, only the specific street frequented by 600,000 people that possesses the capacity to potentially hold them all over the course of a day becomes a *reshus ha'rabbim*. The practical difference relates to side streets in an area that meets Reb Moshe's criteria. According to the *Beis Ephraim*, only the main streets in that area would be precluded from using a *tzuras ha'pesach eruv*.[111] According to Reb Moshe, however, every street (that is at least sixteen *amos* broad) in the area would require doors to allow carrying therein.[112]

5. *Additional Factors in Determining Reshus Ha'Rabbim Status*

There are several other points to ponder regarding whom we count - and in which scenarios we count - the 600,000 people (according to the school of thought that deems this criterion essential in establishing that an area is a *reshus ha'rabbim*).

The first point is that women and children are also included in this tabulation, as are non-Jews.[113] At first glance this seems surprising, as none of these groups was included in the census of individuals suited to serve as soldiers among the Jews who left Egypt - from which we derive this criterion. Several explanations of the rationale for this Halacha are to be found in the *Poskim*.

---

[111] See *Shulchan Aruch*, ibid., 364:1-2 and the *Mishna Berura* 345:27.

[112] See *Igros Moshe*, ibid., 5:28:7. It is not clear whether Reb Moshe holds that each and every (sixteen *amos* wide) street in the area is considered a *reshus ha'rabbim*, or only those that provide access to and from the area.

[113] See *Yesodei Yeshurun*, ibid., pp. 183-184, and *Hilchos Eruvin*, Appendix to Chap. 1, Chapter 5, for the sources that discuss the possibility that the total of 600,000 must be comprised exclusively of Jews, perhaps only of male, adult Jews. No major *Posek* employs this opinion in his formulation of rulings on *eruvin*.

Reb Moshe[114] explains that the 600,000 people that comprised the *reshus ha'rabbim* in the pathways of the camp in the desert were not all men. He estimates that the total population of the camp (including all those excluded from the census) was in the order of a ratio of four or five times 600,000 people. The assumption was that a quarter or a fifth of the total population (including those excluded from the census) was frequently out and about in the public thoroughfares. It was as a result of this calculation that the figure of 600,000 people was fixed as a criterion of *reshus ha'rabbim* - not because this was the total number of men included in the census.[115]

We may suggest another possible explanation based on the *Rashbam*'s statement that the areas of encampment of all the tribes other than *Levi* were not *reshus ha'rabbim.*[116] Only the area occupied by *Shevet Levi* was a *reshus ha'rabbim* - because all the men used to frequent that area to learn Torah from Moshe *Rabbeinu.* It is not that women, children and even non-Jews were not counted. In the particular scenario in the desert from which we derive the criteria of *reshus ha'rabbim*, they were not part of the masses that gathered and comprised those criteria.

---

114 *Igros Moshe*, ibid., 1:139.5.

115 Some rabbinic authorities have interpreted Reb Moshe's intent as follows: In reality, there is no specific requirement of 600,000. The true requirement actually is 2,400,000 to 3,000,000 people - the estimated total of the population of the Jewish camp in the desert. This interpretation leads them to an interesting leniency: Even if we can prove that there are 600,000 people in the streets of a certain area, nevertheless, since the total population of that area does not exceed of 2.4 to 3 million, we cannot classify the area as a *reshus ha'rabbim*. The 600,000 figure, according to this approach, is a "*siman*" (evidence) that 2.4 to 3 million people are present, not a "*sibba*" (reason) to consider an area a *reshus ha'rabbim*. I do not believe that this interpretation is accurate. Careful reading of Reb Moshe's *teshuva* yields the opposite conclusion: The presence of a population of 2.4 to 3 million people in an area is a *siman* that 600,000 people may be found in that area's streets. It is the latter phenomenon that is the *sibba* that the area is considered a *reshus ha'rabbim*. If, therefore, we can prove that more than 600,000 people are in the streets of an area, it is a *reshus ha'rabbim*, even if its population is less than 2.4 to 3 million.

116 *Bava Basra* 60a, *d.h. Vayar es Yisroel*. See above, note 91.

Another important point is the question of whether we include travelers within automobiles in the halachic tally of 600,000. This question first arose in the nineteenth century concerning, then, the status of railroad tracks over which trains carrying a total of more than 600,000 people a day travelled. The *Aruch HaShulchan* rules that train tracks are considered *reshuyos ha'rabbim*.[117] Reb Moshe rules that we also include travelers in cars in the halachic tally of 600,000 people.[118] This is the generally accepted approach.[119]

A final point: It is generally accepted that a sixteen *amos* wide intercity highway is a *reshus ha'rabbim* even if 600,000 people do not travel on it.[120] One of the great Polish *Poskim* of the first half of the

---

117 *Orach Chaim* 345:26. Many respected *Poskim* differed, including the *Beis Ephraim, Orach Chaim, siman* 26; the *Yeshu'os Malko, siman* 27; and, the *Maharsham*, 1:161 and 3:188. See *No'am*, vol. 1, pp. 206-208, and *Hilchos Eruvin*, ibid., 5:4. See also *Nesivos Shabbos* 3:1, note 9 - for the *Shevet HaLevi's* ruling on cablecars.

118 Ibid., at the end of the *teshuva*. It is interesting to note that Rabbi Menachem M. Kasher, one of the major proponents of the Manhattan *eruv*, agreed with Reb Moshe on this point. See *No'am*, ibid., pp. 208-209, cited from Rabbi Kasher's essay in *Torah Sheleima* vol. 15.

119 When, however, I once asked Rabbi Eliezer Yehuda Waldenberg (the *Tzitz Eliezer*) why the Yerushalayim *eruv* includes the Tel Aviv highway, one of the reasons he cited to explain the practice was the opinion that we do not include travelers inside cars in the tally of 600,000. This response astonished me, as I had assumed that this approach was a trademark of *Poskim* of the Galician and Hungarian schools. Subsequently, however, I noted that the *Tikvas Zecharia*, pp. 40-41, also held that travelers in tram and trolley cars do not contribute to the tally of 600,000. We should recall that this work bears the *haskama* of the highly respected Rabbi Yaakov Yosef. Thus, while the great majority of *Poskim* of the Lithuanian school reject the position that we do not count travelers in vehicles when evaluating a street as a *reshus ha'rabbim*, there are a few that do take this concept into account, at least as an additional reason to incline toward leniency where other mitigating factors are involved as well.

120 See *Nesivos Shabbos*, ibid. and *Hilchos Eruvin*, ibid., Chapter 7. Reb Moshe, ibid., holds that, on the contrary, within a city each specific street need not meet the 600,000 requirement on its own. Its status is determined by the twelve by twelve (144) square *mil* tabulation. A highway, on the other hand, must meet the requirement of 600,000 on its own to qualify as a *reshus ha'rabbim*. Reb Moshe interprets the *Shulchan Aruch* in this vein.

twentieth century, Rabbi Shlomo Dovid Kahane, in his 1933 *teshuva* to Paris, notes an halachic irony that stems from this principle:[121] Since it is rare that intercity highways run straight and uninterrupted (*mefulash*) through the inhabited areas of big cities, they generally do not generate problems for large metropolitan areas. Thus, writes Rabbi Kahane, although the *Mishkenos Ya'akov* rejects *eruvin* based on leniencies in the tallying of 600,000 people, it is still rare to find a true *reshus ha'rabbim* in a great city (since their major thoroughfares are not *mefulash*). This, he writes, is the principle upon which the *eruv* in Warsaw was based. Small towns, on the other hand, are often built up around an intercity highway (or, in the last century, train tracks) that runs straight and uninterrupted right through the town, and are, therefore, more susceptible to problems of *reshus ha'rabbim d'oraysa*!

In the United States this Halacha usually does not cause problems in building *eruvin*. Although years ago intercity routes did run freely and directly through towns, at present, most such highways are usually controlled access interstates and the like. The high speeds and heavy traffic that typify such highways usually insure that they are set off from their environs. They are generally either ten *tefachim* lower or higher than the surrounding areas, or bordered by fences that are ten *tefachim* high. We may therefore regard them as distinct, walled-off domains. They, therefore, do not have to be considered when building an *eruv*. We must note, however, two prevalent related problems:[122]

1. Highways <u>do</u> have entrance and exit ramps that break up their "walled-off" status. When a ramp is situated within the *eruv*, *tzuros ha'pesach* must be built to link the end of the embankment or fence on one side of the ramp with the

---

121 The letter was published (with the story of how it was found and some important remarks on the *eruv* in Warsaw) by Rabbi Menachem M. Kasher in *HaPardes* 35:7, and reprinted in *No'am*, vol. 6, p. 34. See, however, *Igros Moshe*, ibid., 5:28:16, where he seems to propose some leniency in minor intercity routes, and even in the less traveled segments of major routes.

122 I am indebted to Rabbi Akiva Yosef Kaplan for noting that the following problems are prevalent and must be highlighted.

beginning of the embankment or fence on the other side. This is true regardless of whether the ramp rises to meet an elevated highway, descends to meet a depressed highway, or traverses flat terrain to meet a highway that is otherwise behind a fence. Furthermore, according to *Noda B'Yehuda*'s ruling that a wall beneath a bridge is rendered invalid by the open road above it, if an "unrectified" ramp rises over the *eruv's tzuras ha'pesach*, it renders the *eruv* invalid![123] (A *tzuras ha'pesach* suffices, because the ramp meets the *reshus ha'rabbim* of the highway at an angle.[124])

2. Since a highway is always considered a *reshus ha'rabbim*, it can only be closed off by doors, not by a *tzuras ha'pesach* (see below, Chapter IV, Section 10). Consequently, even in the case of a depressed highway, the *eruv's tzuras ha'pesach* may not pass over the highway itself. (When, however, an *eruv* connects neighborhoods on either side of a highway, *tzuros ha'pesach* may traverse the highway atop a regular street that crosses the highway on an overpass, as long as they are not over the highway itself.)

6. *The Extraordinary Chazon Ish*

With a most extraordinary and original approach, the *Chazon Ish*[125] provides an halachic basis for the construction of *eruvin* in areas that might otherwise have been precluded from enclosure by an *eruv* Among the basic issues considered in the discussions of the *Gemara* in *Messeches Eruvin* are: a) *asu rabbim u'mivatlei mechitzta* - whether the passage of many people through a wall renders it invalid;[126] and,

---

[123] See above, Chapter I, note 56. Similar conclusions are drawn by Reb Moshe (as we discussed in Chapter I, Section 5) in *Igros Moshe*, ibid., 1:139 and the *Chazon Ish*, ibid., 108:1-6, from the same source, *Eruvin* 84b, *Tosafos d.h. Gag*.

[124] See *Shulchan Aruch*, ibid., 364:1; *Nesivos Shabbos* 21:27; and, above, note 91.

[125] *Orach Chaim*, 107:5-8.

[126] *Eruvin* 20a and 22a.

b) *omed merubeh al ha'parutz k'omed dami* - whether an area whose perimeter is mostly enclosed may be considered wholly enclosed.[127] As we will see (in Chapter IV, Section 6), we unequivocally accept that *asu rabbim u'mivatlei mechitzta* does apply to natural walls. The question we will discuss here is whether this principle extends to artificial barriers as well.

The issue of *asu rabbim u'mivatlei mechitzta* is argued by two *Amoraim*. Rabbi Yochanan holds that the passage of many people through a wall renders it invalid; Rabbi Eliezer disagrees. The *Mishna Berura*[128] explains that this disagreement has major halachic

---

127 *Eruvin* 16b. See above, Chapter I, Section 3.

128 *Bi'ur Halacha* 364:1, *d.h. Ve'Achar She'asa La*. See also *Avodas Avoda* on the *Avodas HaKodesh* 2:4, note 46. The definition of the traversing *rabbim* (masses) necessary to invalidate an enclosure according to Rabbi Yochanan is a major, unresolved, issue. The *Aruch HaShulchan*, ibid., 353:50, seems to hold that the definition of *rabbim* that are *mivatlei mechitzta* is the same amount as that which creates a *reshus ha'rabbim*. This would mean that only a street that already has the problem of *reshus ha'rabbim* will have the problem of *asu rabbim u'mivatlei mechitzta*. He seems, however, to contradict this position later (ibid., 354:1). See *Nesivos Shabbos* 25:11 and notes 42-45.

The *Poskim* who are inclined to be lenient note that the *Rambam, Hilchos Shabbos* 17:33 evidently rules according to Rabbi Eliezer, as we will explain here briefly. While an exhaustive review of the sources and the process that led the *Rambam* to his ruling is beyond the scope of our discussion, we must note some additional material:

There is a link between the dispute between Rabbi Yochanan and Rabbi Eliezer and an earlier dispute, among the *Tana'im*, between Rabbi Yehuda and *Rabbanan* (the other Sages), as to the underlying basis of the device of "*pasei bira'os*" ("boards surrounding wells"). This dispute, in *Eruvin* 22a (see also 20a), concerns an enclosure consisting of four two-sided posts (of at least an *amah* width in each direction and ten *tefachim* height), which, taken together, form the corners of a square (fig. 10, see overleaf). The purpose of this enclosure was to allow travellers to Yerushalayim for the *Yomim Tovim* who had to camp on the road over *Shabbos* to access wells - that, because of their dimensions were *reshuyos ha'yachid* (see above, Chapter I, Section 2) - on *Shabbos*. The *pasei bira'os* served to enclose an area around the well and render it a *reshus ha'yachid*. (There are several criteria that must be met in order to utilize *pasei bira'os*, see *Nesivos Shabbos* Chap. 14. Nevertheless, when and whether one may make use of them in practice is a separate question from whether they create a *reshus ha'yachid d'oraysa* in the area that they enclose. They do indeed, regardless of whether there is an actual well in the enclosed area or not.)

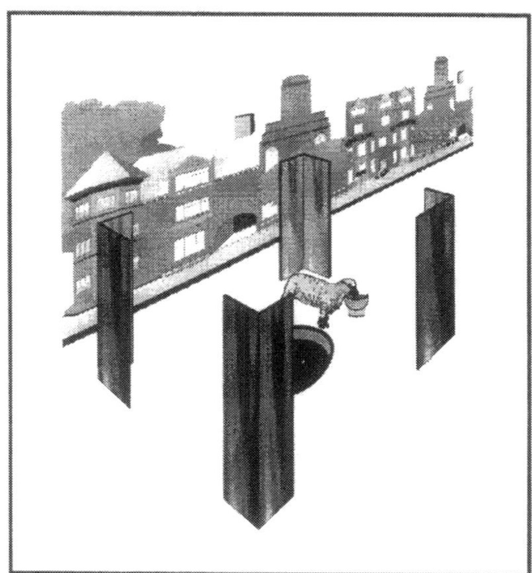

Fig. 10

Rabbi Yehuda held that *pasei bira'os* were not effective if they were positioned in the middle of a *reshus ha'rabbim*, because *asu rabbim u'mevatlei mechitzta*. *Rabbanan* were of the opinion that the *pasei bira'os* are even effective when positioned in the middle of a *reshus ha'rabbim*, because *lo asu rabbim u'mevatlei mechitzta*. The aforementioned *Rambam* follows the opinion of *Rabbanan* and Rabbi Eliezer. Other *Rishonim* disagree. For example, the *Hashlama* (printed in the Shabsai Frankel edition - Yerushalayim, 1975 - of the *Yad HaChazaka*) decides in favor of Rabbi Yehuda and Rabbi Yochanan's opinion. Hence, according to the *Rambam*, the requirement for doors on a *reshus ha'rabbim* that has valid *tzuros ha'pesach* - or any other form of enclosure that suffices *me'd'oraysa* - is only *d'rabbanan*: Since, *me'd'oraysa*, the masses travelling through a wall do not invalidate it, a requirement to impede their movement must, perforce, be *d'rabbanan* - see *Chazon Ish*, ibid., 74:1-3.

The *Mishkenos Ya'akov*, in accordance with his view that the Halacha follows Rabbi Yochanan's opinion, denies that the *Rambam's* intent is to rule according to *Rabbanan* and Rabbi Eliezer. He asserts that the *Rambam* may have meant only to allow *pasei bira'os* on a highway that is not a true *reshus ha'rabbim* (*Orach Chaim siman* 121, p. 119 in the Sheinberger -Yerushalayim 1960 - edition). He concedes, however, that none of the *Rishonim* understood the *Rambam* in this vein. Rather, they all understood that the *Rambam* accepted the views of *Rabbanan* and Rabbi Eliezer.

consequences. If we were to accept Rabbi Yochanan's approach, it is likely that almost no urban *tzuras ha'pesach eruv* would be valid. Utility poles must inevitably cross over city streets, and the *Mishna Berura* posits that city streets fall into the category of *asu rabbim*. Only if we can rely on the approach of Rabbi Eliezer may such *tzuras ha'pesach eruvin* be valid - in his view, the masses do not invalidate the enclosure. The *Rishonim* do not provide a definite unambiguous ruling on this issue. It is, therefore, one of the subjects of the conflict between the *Mishkenos Ya'akov* - who decides in favor of Rabbi Yochanan's opinion; and the *Beis Ephraim* - who decides in favor of Rabbi Eliezer's opinion. The *Mishna Berura* writes that the lack of a clearcut lenient decision in the *Rishonim* is another reason that a *Ba'al Nefesh* should not rely on urban *tzuras ha'pesach eruvin*. The *Aruch HaShulchan*[129] and *Chazon Ish*,[130] however, both accept the ruling of the *Beis Ephraim* and rule, in practice: *lo asu rabbim u'mivatlei mechitzta*.

Let us examine how the issue of *omed merubeh al ha'parutz k'omed dami* concerns us. In its basic sense this principle means that an area that is, say, ten *amos* by ten *amos* square (100 square *amos*), that, thus, has a perimeter of forty *amos*, is considered halachically enclosed if, of that perimeter, a total of at least twenty-one *amos* (somewhat more than five *amos* of wall on each side of the perimeter[131]) is walled. The entire enclosed area is a *reshus ha'yachid d'oraysa*. *Me'd'rabbanan*, if any single break in the wall of a city is wider than ten *amos*, it requires an additional rectification - a *tzuras ha'pesach*, etc.

Now let us analyze a case where a true *reshus ha'rabbim*, such as a highway, runs through a break in the wall. There is no doubt that at least *me'd'rabbanan* such a break requires some rectification, since this *reshus ha'rabbim* is by definition more than ten *amos* (at least sixteen *amos*) wide. The question, however, is, does this *reshus*

---

129 Ibid.

130 Ibid.

131 See below, Chapter IV, note 167.

ha'rabbim even negate the *omed merubeh al ha'parutz* enclosure on a *d'oraysa* level? The *Mishkenos Ya'akov* proves from the *Gemara*'s discussions of Yerushalayim[132] that in such a situation the enclosure is, indeed, invalidated on a *d'oraysa* level. Yerushalayim was surrounded by *omed merubeh* walls, yet, nevertheless, the breaks in the wall rendered the city a *reshus ha'rabbim me'd'oraysa*. The *Mishkenos Ya'akov* concludes that the principle of *omed merubeh al ha'parutz k'omed dami* does not apply to cases where the breaks in the wall include streets that fall into the category of *reshus ha'rabbim*.

The *Chazon Ish* rejects the proof from Yerushalayim. The statement, that if not for its doors Yerushalayim would have been considered a *reshus ha'rabbim*, was made by Rabbi Yochanan, who holds *asu rabbim u'mivatlei mechitzta*, thus negating the *omed merubeh* here. The *Chazon Ish*, of course, rules in accordance with Rabbi Eliezer's opinion that *lo asu rabbim u'mivatlei mechitzta*. Consequently, even if Yerushalayim had not had doors, the *omed merubeh* would have assured that it was a *reshus ha'yachid d'oraysa*.[133]

---

132 *Eruvin* 6b.

133 Rabbi Akiva Yosef Kaplan noted that the first *Tosafos HaRosh* in the second *perek* of *Messeches Eruvin*, 17b, *d.h. Arba'ah Deyumdin* is essentially an explicit endorsement of the *Chazon Ish*. The *Rosh* there writes that wherever there exist four halachic walls - even if *parutz merubeh al ha'omed*, such as in the case of *pasei bira'os* (see above, note 128) - a break in the walls - even one that is wider than ten *amos* - only disrupts the enclosure *me'd'rabbanan* (see, however, the first *Ritva* in the second *perek, d.h. Ha Kasivna*, and below, note 134).

There is another *Gemara* about Yerushalayim that troubles the *Chazon Ish*. The *Gemara* in *Eruvin* 101a states that, after the wall of Yerushalayim was broken in several places, the city became a *reshus ha'rabbim*. The *Chazon Ish* asks: Was the wall so broken that it was no longer *omed merubeh*? He proposes approaches too technical for the scope of our discussion.

Let us note that this passage is not just difficult for the *Chazon Ish*. *Rabbeinu* Chananel there says that the breaks in the walls of Yerushalayim were each more than ten *amos* broad. That is the minimum dimension for a break in a wall to require a rectification of some sort, but it is not a sufficient dimension for the break to constitute a *reshus ha'rabbim* - a thoroughfare must be at least sixteen *amos* wide to be a *reshus ha'rabbim*. (Although a thoroughfare that is generally sixteen *amos* wide but in one place narrows to less than sixteen *amos* may be considered still a *reshus ha'rabbim*, it is not clear if this is the case where it goes through a wall. Furthermore, it may still have to retain a width of thirteen and a third *amos*. See the *Nesivos Shabbos* 3:3; above, Chapter I, note 65; and, below, note 134.)

Perhaps we can find a simpler solution to this enigma than those proposed there by the *Chazon Ish*. We will see below (Chapter IV, Section 10) that there are two ways in which to understand the efficacy of doors in enclosing a *reshus ha'rabbim*. The *Chazon Ish* holds that doors are an extension of the principle of *tzuras ha'pesach*. Others, however, hold that doors are of a different character, that they serve to block traffic.

The *Rashba* (*Avodas HaKodesh* 3:1) - and others, see the *Avodas Avoda* there note 2 - holds that there are halachic distinctions between the two types of *reshus ha'rabbim* mentioned in the *Gemara*: A *"sratya"* - thoroughfare - and a *"platya"* - central public square or market. While doors serve to block a thoroughfare and render it a *reshus ha'yachid*, they do not render a public square a *reshus ha'yachid*. The generally accepted understanding of the *Rashba*'s position is that a *platya* is not a *reshus ha'rabbim* because of a high volume of traffic - which may, indeed, be prevented by doors - but, rather, by the presence of a static multitude - upon which doors obviously have no impact. According to the *Rashba*, even when Yerushalayim was fully walled and doored, the public squares within the city retained their character as *reshuyos ha'rabbim* and carrying remained prohibited in those areas (although not in other streets of the city, as noted by the *Sefer HaBattim, Sha'ar Sha'arei Issur Hotza'a* 1:15 in his explanation of the *Rashba*'s position).

Most sources argue with the *Rashba*, and the final, accepted ruling is that *delasos* are effective in rendering a *platya* a *reshus ha'yachid*. (See the *Avodas Avoda*, ibid., that even the *Rashba* may concede the point where the *platya* itself - as opposed to the surrounding city - is surrounded by doors, as the *Meiri* (*Shabbos* 6a) states:

> What is a *reshus ha'rabbim*? A *sratya*, which is a roadway that runs from city to city; and a *platya*, which is a square in which the masses gather to transact business. Even if the *platya* is not open, and even if the doors of the district are closed at night, nevertheless, if the *platya* itself does not have doors [it is always considered a *reshus ha'rabbim*]. Were it to have doors, however, then, as any *reshus ha'rabbim*, it would be considered enclosed and subject to an *eruv*.... And that which they said (*Eruvin* 6b) that Yerushalayim, were its doors not closed at night, would have been considered a *reshus ha'rabbim*, which implies that when there were doors to the city that closed there was no *d'oraysa* prohibition on carrying within the city, i.e., that no places within it - even the *platyos* - were considered *reshuyos ha'rabbim*, should not be understood that way. Rather, the streets that were broad and serviced multitudes as common domains were broken by doors. The *platyos* in the city that were sixteen *amos* wide, however, remained *reshuyos ha'rabbim* even when the city has closable doors.

(The *Meiri* attributes this understanding to the *"Gedolei HaDor"* - "The Great

The *Chazon Ish* does concede a point to the *Mishkenos Ya'akov*. He admits that a *reshus ha'rabbim* does negate an *omed merubeh*, but only where the *reshus ha'rabbim* is *"mefulash,"* i.e., where it follows a continuous, straight, uninterrupted line through the city. If, however, a street that would otherwise be a *reshus ha'rabbim* is obstructed at some point by a wall or building that either ends the street or causes it to deviate significantly from a straight line, it loses its status of *reshus ha'rabbim d'oraysa*. When a building obstructs the street, etc. (fig. 11) then that building becomes, in essence, its third wall - qualifying the street as a *reshus ha'yachid d'oraysa*.

Based on these two foundations, the *Chazon Ish* builds an extraordinary proposition: A city in which at least one street ends in

---

Ones of the Generation" - his pseudonym for the *Rashba*.)

Nevertheless, the *Rashba*'s logic seems sound - if doors are meant to block traffic - as the *Rashba* writes - how do they serve to enclose a *platya*, where traffic is not the issue?

It seems reasonable to posit that the purpose of doors on the *platya* is not to block traffic, but rather, <u>to create a perfect enclosure</u>. It seems that *omed merubeh al ha'parutz* walls - even, as *Rabbeinu* Chananel notes, walls that leave openings of less than sixteen *amos* - are not sufficient to render a public square a *reshus ha'yachid*. This is because the nature of a public square is such that as long as access is provided in some way, it can serve its purpose as a gathering place for multitudes. It is only when it is within our capacity to completely deny access to the *platya* by means of a halachically perfect enclosure (breaks of less than ten *amos* and doors on those breaks that are more than ten *amos* wide - <u>even though they are not sixteen *amos* wide</u>) that the *reshus ha'rabbim* status of a *platya* is eliminated.

Thus, the reason that Yerushalayim was considered a *reshus ha'rabbim* after its wall was broken was not because of the thoroughfares <u>through</u> the wall, but rather because of the public squares <u>within</u> the wall. *Omed merubeh al ha'parutz* walls would not render a city with major central marketplaces and squares a *reshus ha'yachid*, only perfect enclosures could serve this purpose.

(We must note that although the *Chacham Tzvi* in his *teshuva* on England - *siman* 37 - expresses bewilderment over the *Shulchan Aruch*'s omission of the *Rashba*'s opinion, the accepted Halacha is that a *platya* that is within a completely walled and doored city is rendered a *reshus ha'yachid me'd'oraysa* even if the *platya* is not enclosed by its own walls and doors. Not that this leniency is particularly relevant to modern metropolitan *eruvin* - since they generally do not consist of true walls and doors they may not, in any event, contain any area that might be defined as a *platya*.)

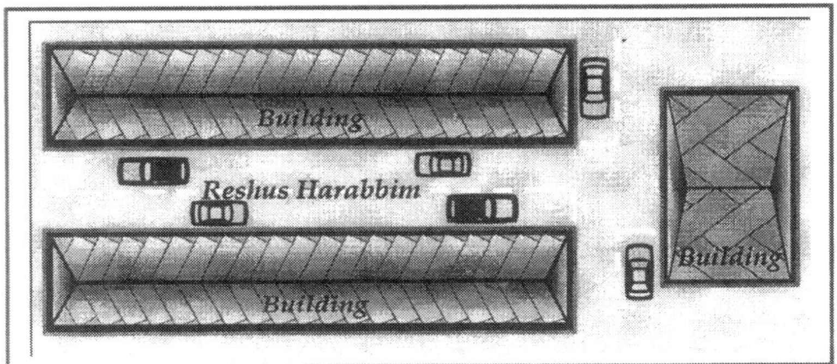

Fig. 11

an obstructed dead end does not have a *reshus ha'rabbim d'oraysa*!

Let us examine the scene that the *Chazon Ish* himself draws (fig. 12). The *Chazon Ish* writes:

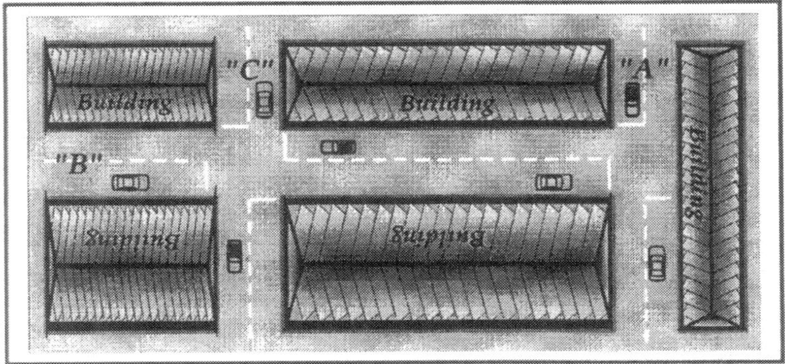

Fig. 12

In such a case we will not find a *reshus ha'rabbim* [*d'oraysa*] even if the streets are sixteen *amos* wide and 600,000 people traverse them. 'B' Street is a true *reshus ha'yachid d'oraysa*. It has three walls of *omed merubeh*. Although: a) 'A' St. and 'C' St. pass through breaks in the "walls" of 'B' St.; and, b) the fact that *rabbim* traverse these streets, nevertheless, the walls are not negated. A break of ten or more *amos* in an enclosure precludes carrying in that enclosed area only *me'd'rabbanan. Me'd'oraysa* no break in an enclosure that is *omed merubeh* can negate the enclosure.

Since 'B' St. is now a *reshus ha'yachid,* 'A' St. and 'C' St. become *reshuyos ha'yachid* as well. They, too, now possess three walls: The points at which they each open into 'B' St. are now considered halachically sealed - as if by walls - by [the *omed merubeh* walls of] 'B' St., that is now halachically regarded as a courtyard surrounded by walls on three sides...

In a case, however, where there are only two [intersecting] streets, such as where 'B' St. and 'C' St. intersect and there is no building at the end of 'B' St., we cannot employ the principle of *omed merubeh.* We can only utilize *omed merubeh* where each *"omed"* can create a *reshus ha'yachid* on its own [i.e., some structure pre-exists on each of three sides and we are only using *omed merubeh* to fill the gaps].

The *Chazon Ish* concludes:

We conclude from this that in our day and age all the marketplaces and roads, even in the greatest metropolises, are really *reshuyos ha'yachid d'oraysa.* In every city you will find [at least] one street enclosed by three walls that is, therefore, a *reshus ha'yachid d'oraysa.* All the streets that intersect this street also become *reshuyos ha'yachid.* We may therefore rectify them with *tzuros ha'pesach* [as opposed to the *delasos* required for *reshus ha'rabbim*]. The *Mishna Berura* in *siman* 345 wrote at length about how difficult it is to be lenient based [only on the opinion that if] less than 600,000 people travel on a highway upon which many people travel and do business [it is still not defined as a *reshus ha'rabbim*]. According, however, to what has just been clarified, the basis for leniency in our cities is clear and broad.

Other *Acharonim* (including Reb Moshe)[134] disagree with the

134 *Igros Moshe,* ibid., 5:28:3. See *Nesivos Shabbos* 3:1 note 8 and 23:2, note 14, and below, Chapter IV, note 165. Whether a *pirtza* wider than ten *amos* interrupts *omed merubeh* was yet another topic disputed by the *Mishkenos Ya'akov* and

Chazon Ish, but the *Chazon Ish*'s great stature, especially in *Hilchos Eruvin*, lends considerable credence to his views.[135]

7. Chapter Conclusion

We have seen many conflicting approaches to the issue of defining *reshus ha'rabbim* in modern metropolitan areas. As we have already stated, it is not our intention here to render practical halachic decisions. We hope that the reader now understands the dimensions of the problems and the rationales underlying the various positions involved in this matter. We also hope that we have now better equipped the reader to reach - in consultation with *Poskim* and rabbinic authorities - an halachically valid approach toward the problems involved in the construction or use of an *eruv* in any city - lived in or visited.

Beis Ephraim.

Rabbi Akiva Yosef Kaplan noted that, although he does not cite the *Chazon Ish* explicitly, Rabbi Aharon Kotler, in *Mishnas Rabbi Aharon* 1:6:2:1-8, is inclined to accept the contention of the *Mishkenos Ya'akov*, that a break wider than ten *amos* does interrupt *omed merubeh al ha'parutz*. He bases his position on the *Rabbeinu Chananel* that we discussed above, in note 134. Reb Aharon interprets *Rashi, Eruvin* 94a, *d.h. Chatzer She'nifratza*, on the basis of the *Mishkenos Ya'akov*'s contention as well. *Rashi* there seems to indicate that a *reshus ha'rabbim* may narrow to a width of ten *amos* yet still retain its character as a *reshus ha'rabbim*. Rabbi Chaim Twerski remarked to me that, nevertheless, it is not clear that *Rashi* would agree with *Rabbeinu Chananel*, as *Rabbeinu Chananel* is discussing the walls of Yerushalayim, that were, in all likelihood, *omed merubeh*, while *Rashi* is discussing the walls surrounding a courtyard, that may well, at least on the side bordering on the *reshus ha'rabbim*, not be *omed merubeh*.

Rabbi Kaplan also noted that Rabbi Eliezer Plachinsky's *Shalom Yehuda, siman* 33, contains an extensive correspondence between the author and the *Chazon Ish*, concerning the latter's *chiddush* that we have discussed here.

135 For an example of the *Chazon Ish* serving as an authority on the Halachos of *eruvin* even for a *Posek HaDor*, see the *Achi'ezer*, ibid., where Rabbi Chaim Ozer Grodziensky notes that he based his approval of an *eruv* in Paris in part on communications with the *Chazon Ish*. We should note, however, that this *teshuva* does not employ the *chiddush* of the *Chazon Ish* that we have discussed here.

The distinction between the situation in Israel and that in North America should now be obvious. In Israel, until very recently, no cities were of the size necessary to fulfill the criterion of 600,000 as interpreted by Reb Moshe and others. Few streets were of the size necessary to meet the criterion of *reshus ha'rabbim* according to the *Beis Ephraim*. Furthermore, in *Eretz Yisroel*, to a great extent, the rulings of the *Chazon Ish* carry decisive weight. Thus, the potential for controversy was, and still remains, relatively small. In *Chutz La'aretz*, however, many cities were - already early in the halachic history of North America - and are of the size necessary to fulfill the criterion of 600,000 as interpreted by Reb Moshe. Many streets were, and are, of the size necessary to meet the criterion of *reshus ha'rabbim* according to the *Beis Ephraim*. The potential for controversy (in inverse proportion to the amount of opinions one may rely upon in building or using an urban *eruv*) was, and is, therefore, dramatically enhanced.

Chapter IV

THE CONSTRUCTION OF ERUVIN IN URBAN AREAS

1. How an Urban Tzuras Ha'Pesach is Built

A *Posek* once took my *chavrusa* and me on a field trip around the *eruv* of an urban community. He brought us to a specific street marked on the *eruv* map as the border of the *eruv*. He offered to give us each $10.00 if we were successful at identifying the lines of the *eruv*. We did not earn those $10.00! It might be a surprise to anyone who has built a backyard *eruv* to realize that building a communal *eruv* usually entails little installation of wire. For the most part, resourceful *eruv* committees spend weeks and months identifying pre-existing structures to serve as part of the communal enclosure. Concern over funds or municipal regulations often makes it expedient to use pre-existing structures. Urban *eruvin*, therefore, often follow seemingly illogical patterns, separating sidewalks from streets, cutting through alleys, or encompassing broad areas with few Jews, specifically in order to utilize pre-existing structures. These structures are often actual walls: fences, embankments, riverbanks, sides of buildings, etc. If these wall-like structures are man-made, they, generally, pose few problems. (Let us stress that word: "few"- we will return later to explore some possible problems.)

Urban *eruvin* almost inevitably, however, incorporate long spans of overhead cable and the poles to which this cable is attached. Nowadays, these cables and poles generally belong to the electric or telephone utility companies. A century and a half ago, when these cables and poles were first discussed in halachic sources (see above, Chapter I, Section 3), they were, of course, telegraph lines, and they are often referred to as such even today. It is the use of overhead cable that causes most of the problems encountered in contemporary urban *eruvin*.

Initially, the very concept of a telegraph line as a *tzuras ha'pesach* encountered resistance. Could a structure not meant as a doorway serve as an halachic doorway? After all, telegraph lines were not meant to serve as doorways. Some *Poskim* countered that: a) the lines were raised on poles above ground; and, b) the poles were never placed right in the middle of a street or sidewalk, precisely in order to afford easy passage through the "doorways" thus formed. Others ruled that the intention of the Jewish population to incorporate the telegraph lines in an *eruv* itself sufficed to redesignate them as doorways.[136] In practice, for well over a century the use of telegraph lines and their successor electric and telephone lines has been commonplace and universal.

The most basic Halacha of *tzuras ha'pesach*, the door frame effect that *Halacha l'Moshe me'Sinai* (the unbroken chain of tradition in Halacha from Sinai)[137] recognizes as a wall, is that the cable (the *"kaneh she'al gabeihem"*) which crosses over the poles (the *"lechayayim"* - singular: *"lechi"*) must pass over the top of the poles, not on or over the sides of the poles. Crossing over the side of the poles constitutes the problem of *"tzuras ha'pesach min hatzad,"* "a door frame on the side," explicitly invalidated by the *Gemara* in *Eruvin* (fig. 13).[138]

---

136 See the *Tikvas Zecharia*, pp.28-31; *Yesodei Yeshurun*, vol. 2, pp. 268-269; and, *Nesivos Shabbos* 19:12 and note 29, who does not even mention the dissenting opinion in his formulation of the Halachos. See below note 137.

137 See *Sukkah* 5b.

138 *Eruvin* 5a, *Shulchan Aruch, Orach Chaim* 362:11.

One of the early metropolitan *eruvin* in North America was that of Toronto. The original *eruv*, in the downtown area (no longer inhabited by the Jewish community) was constructed by a great Polish *Posek*, Rabbi Yehuda Leib Graubart, the *Chavalim b'Ne'emeem*. Rabbi Graubart theorized that cables on crossbars and similar structures (such as are found on the metal structures that support high tension wires) do not fall into the category of *tzuras ha'pesach min hatzad*. He suggests that a *tzuras ha'pesach min hatzad* only exists where a cable is literally bolted to the side of a pole. Where, however, the cable is attached to the top of a crossbar, it is not technically a *tzuras ha'pesach min hatzad* - see *Chavalim b'Ne'emeem* 3:14-19 and *Yesodei Yeshurun*, ibid., pp. 278-280. There were also *Acharonim* who ruled that *"b'she'as ha'dechak"* (at times when oppressive circumstances exert pressure to incline to leniency) it is possible to rely with overhead cables on *tzuras ha'pesach min hatzad*.

Fig. 13

This Halacha poses a formidable problem when using overhead cable in the construction of an *eruv*. Occasionally the cable does in fact go from the top of one pole to the top of the next. More often, however, the cable is attached to the side of the pole. Frequently, the same cable will weave back and forth, going from the top of the pole to the side of the next one, out on a crossbar and back again in quick succession![139]

The vast majority of *Poskim*, however, resoundingly reject this position. See *Hilchos Eruvin* (Tel Aviv, 1972) 4:5-8, notes 67-68, and Rabbi Ovadia Yosef's *haskama* to the *sefer* (see also *Nesivos Shabbos* 19:31, note 70 and 19:41, note 91).

Furthermore, it is difficult to conceive of a true *she'as ha'dechak* in our circumstances. In 19th century Europe an *eruv* was often essential to bring water to one's house on *Shabbos*! In a *teshuva* written to Detroit in 1979, Rabbi Moshe Feinstein discusses what is considered a "*tzorech*" (need) and/or "*tzorech gadol*" that would indicate that an *eruv* should be built in a community. See *Igros Moshe, Orach Chaim* 5:29 (and the end of the preceding *teshuva* there as well). "*Tzorech gadol*" is not, however, license to build and rely upon a "*she'as ha'dechak eruv.*" See also below note 22. Normative Halacha, and current practice, is never to allow the use of *tzuras ha'pesach min hatzad*.

An interesting tangent: The *Maharsham* 4:71 is of the opinion that the *chuppa* (canopy) used at wedding ceremonies must be defined as surrounded by halachic walls. He writes that, therefore, *tzuras ha'pesach min hatzad* is unacceptable, and that, therefore, it is essential that the poles be underneath the canopy, not to the sides of the canopy - see *Nesivos Shabbos* 19:28, note 63.

139 Frequently the overhead cable will run through a hole drilled into a wooden utility pole (known as a "bolt-through" pole). The use of such poles and cables as part of a *tzuras ha'pesach* hinges on a disagreement between the *Mishna Berura* 362:64 (*l'chumra*) and the *Aruch HaShulchan, Orach Chaim*, 362:32 and *Chazon Ish, Orach Chaim*, 71:9 (*l'kulla*) about whether the *lechi* may extend above the

In Israel, where the municipal authorities are more cooperative, the problem of *tzuras ha'pesach min hatzad* is often easily rectified. Wide barrels that are at least ten *tefachim* high are placed underneath the overhead cable. The halachic principle of *"gud asek mechitzta"* (literally: extend the walls up) then creates imaginary lines directly up from the top of the barrel to the cable.[140] These imaginary lines may be drawn from any point on the top of the barrel. If any of these imaginary lines hit the cable overhead, we may view the barrel, not the utility pole, as the *lechi* for the *tzuras ha'pesach* (fig. 14).

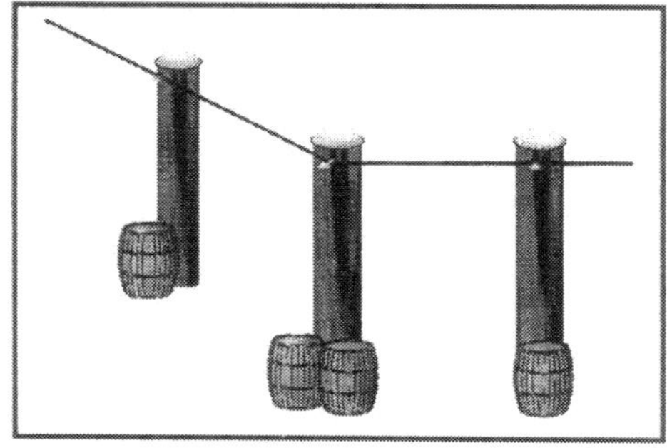

Fig. 14

In the diaspora, however, the authorities are not as cooperative, and will usually not allow such obtrusive rectifications. A routine approach here is, therefore, to bolt much narrower objects, such as a plank, a rod, or tubing, to utility poles to serve as *lechayayim*.[141]

---

cable or not. See also *Nesivos Shabbos* 19:31 and note 70; and *Hilchos Eruvin* 4:3 and note 62 (these sources are inclined to be lenient in this scenario). This author once had occasion to inquire as to the status of high voltage towers where one of the wires ran through the tower. The *Poskim* contacted were not inclined to regard the crisscrossing metal bars that comprised the tower's structure as sufficiently similar to the solid beam of a utility pole, and would not permit the use of such towers without further rectification.

140 See *Mishna Berura*, ibid., *se'if katan* 62. The *Pri Megadim* 363:19 states that there may not be a gap of twenty *amos* between the top of the barrel or other object used as a *lechi* and the overhead cable. (It is not clear whether this *chumra* is universally accepted *l'halacha*.)

141 It may be possible to use stripes consisting of thick paint or reflector strips as *lechayayim*. The advantage of such *lechayayim* is that they are more resistant to vandalism. The validity of this solution involves the Halacha in *Shulchan Aruch*, ibid., 362:11 that the *tzuras ha'pesach* must be strong enough to support a door made of straw. While painted stripes or reflector strips only possess such strength

2. *Problems Encountered in the Use of a Rod as a Lechi*

The problem most frequently encountered in the use of a narrow object as *lechi* is in the application of *gud asek*. The *Chazon Ish* rules explicitly that the imaginary line is always drawn straight up, no matter the angle of the *lechi*.[142] No creditable *Posek* has ever ruled otherwise. Yet many utility poles are warped or bent at an angle. This may occur either because of carelessness in the original construction, weather conditions over time, or jolts by cars or trucks. The *lechayayim* attached to such poles bend with them at the same angle. *Gud asek*, however, still draws the imaginary line straight up from the top of the *lechi* (fig. 15)![143] In this situation the *gud asek* is meaningless, as the line drawn from the top of the *lechi* will not hit the overhead cable. Despite this halachic peril, some rabbinic authorities will, nevertheless, allow the use of *gud asek lechayayim* in the construction of an *eruv* based on utility poles. They attempt to prevent the bent pole problem by employing a surveyor's tool or plumb line to determine whether the *lechi* is directly underneath the overhead cable. At best, however, this is a hazardous approach. Even one flawed *lechi* may invalidate an entire

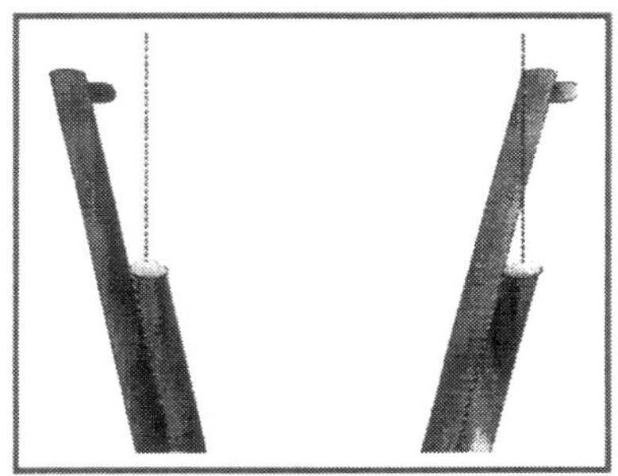

Fig. 15

---

together with the surface upon which they are painted, the *Mishna Berura* 363:26 allows such *lechayayim* if they possess some substance. See also *Nesivos Shabbos* 19:24.

142 Ibid., 71:6. See *Hilchos Eruvin* 4:13 and note 82. The *Aruch HaShulchan*, ibid., 363:46 also states explicitly that the cable must be directly "absolutely straight" over the *lechayayim*.

143 The left-hand diagram in fig. 15 shows a cable drawn across the top of the slant of a *lechi*. The *Chazon Ish*, ibid., rules that *gud asek* begins only at the top, not the middle of a pole. The *Avnei Nezer, Orach Chaim*, 291:12 proposes a novel approach to such a case, that the later *Poskim* question. See *Hilchos Eruvin* 4:13 note 82 and *Nesivos Shabbos* 19:39, note 86.

eruv! A typical urban *eruv* may contain hundreds of *lechayayim* attached to telephone poles. The surveyor (usually a utility company employee or a hastily trained member of the local *eruv* committee) must meticulously check every pole. This can be a time consuming, tedious, and sometimes expensive task. Unless one's *yiras shomayim* (fear of Heaven) is very strong, diligence tends to erode over time. Any pole may bend over time, requiring constant surveillance.[144]

Another problem may arise when *gud asek lechayayim* are used. Often a utility company box may be attached to the utility pole between the *lechi* and the overhead cable. If the *lechi* is built all the way up to the box, or to within three *tefachim* of it, then the box may be considered part of the *lechi*. The halachic mechanism of "*lavud*" connects them (see Section 3 below). If, however, the *lechi* ends more than three *tefachim* beneath the box, then the box interrupts the *gud asek*.[145]

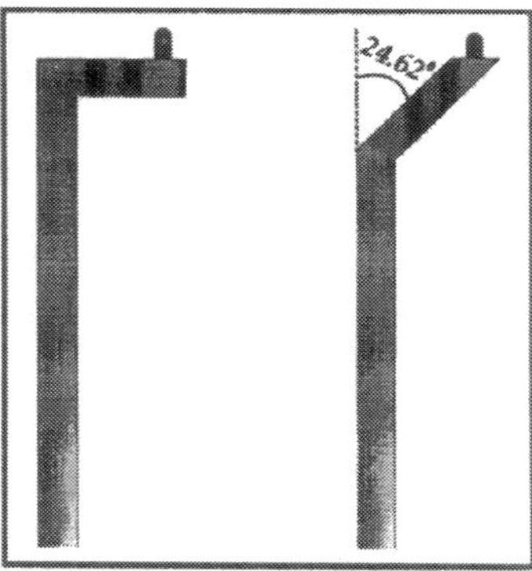

Fig. 16

Due to all these considerations,

---

144 In the first edition of this work I noted here a remark of one of my *Rabbeim* that, like most Halachos in Torah, we must render decisions here based on the perspective of the naked eye - whether that perspective leads one to a more stringent or more lenient conclusion (see *Michtav Me'Eliyahu* vol. 4 pp. 355-356, note 4). Rabbi Shlomo Miller, however, in his *haskama* to this work, and others, took issue with the application of this principle to *Hilchos Eruvin*. I therefore consulted that *Rebbe*, and he informed me that he did not mean his original remark as a practical ruling, and directed me to remove it from the text.

145 *Mishna Berura* 363:112 based on the *Taz* there *se'if katan* 19. The scenario discussed there concerns a roof positioned between the *lechi* and the overhead cable, but it seems that the same Halacha applies to this case. I am indebted to Rabbi Chaim Moshe Levy who found this ruling explicit in the *Divrei Yechezkel siman* 6 and cited a similar *psak* in the *Avnei Nezer*, ibid., *siman* 231. See also *Halachos of the Eruv* Chap. VII, I; and *Nesivos Shabbos* 19:27 and note 62. Sometimes, however, a problem of *pischei shima'ei* may be involved. See below, Section 3.

"state of the art" *eruvin* do not utilize *gud asek lechayayim*, but, rather, build the *lechayayim* all the way up to the overhead cable. No imaginary lines need then be drawn, as an actual structure extends all the way to the wire. Actual structures constructed on an angle are halachically valid.[146]

3. *Problems with the Overhead Cable*

The *Mishna Berura* notes a major disagreement about whether the cable must be absolutely taut or may sag and/or sway in the wind between the *lechayayim* (fig. 17).[147] The trend, based on the *Aruch HaShulchan* and others, is

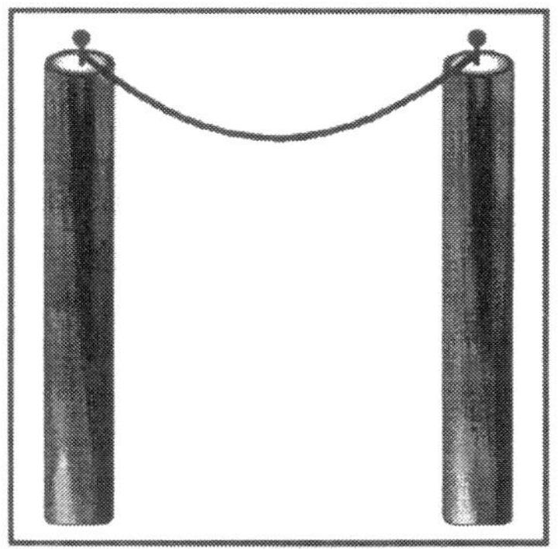

Fig. 17

146 *Chazon Ish* and *Hilchos Eruvin*, ibid., The *lechi* itself, however, must be reasonably straight, not pronouncedly crooked or bent (any angle of more than approximately 25 degrees is problematic) (fig. 16). Otherwise, questions of *pischei shima'ei* and other problems may be involved. See below, end of Section 3; *Chazon Ish*, ibid., 71:11; and *Hilchos Eruvin* 3:13 and notes 83-84. See *Halachos of the Eruv* Chap. VII, C; *Hilchos Eruvin* 3:10; and *Nesivos Shabbos*, ibid., for discussions of overhead cables on an angle (i.e., where one supporting *lechi* is higher than the other). Rabbi Eider cites a *psak* from Rabbi Aharon Kotler that an angle of more than 45 degrees upwards or downwards is problematic. The *Nesivos Shabbos* 19:27 note 60 questions whether this might be too great a leniency and is loathe to allow an angle greater than that of a *tel hamislaket* (see below, Section 7).

There are many possible shapes that may render *lechayayim* invalid. These include *lechayayim* shaped like a sideways "U"; *lechayayim* shaped like the Hebrew letter *"tzaddi sofis"* (ץ); *lechayayim* that sit atop other structures, such as a tripod; *lechayayim* that consist of more than one board or rod, nailed or joined in a way that the one atop which the overhead cable runs is not directly over the other one; etc. While these scenarios are rare, it is important to be on the alert and insure that they do not occur! See *Hilchos Eruvin* 3:14 and *Nesivos Shabbos* 19:27-43 for diagrams and rulings on these and many other variations.

147 362:66; see *Nesivos Shabbos* 19:42. See also Rabbi Tzvi Pesach Frank's *Har Tzvi, Orach Chaim* vol. 2, *siman* 18:8 and *siman* 19 for a significant leniency in this area.

to be lenient:[148] If when there is no wind the cable at rest runs due straight from *lechi* to *lechi* the *eruv* is valid.

As we have noted, overhead cables often weave back and forth. A characteristic question concerns the following case (fig. 18): Three utility poles, each consisting of an upright pole and a crossbar across the top, stand in a row. The overhead cable runs directly across the first and third pole in the row, but is connected to the crossbar of the middle pole. Here, even when at rest, the cable does not run directly from *lechi* to *lechi*.

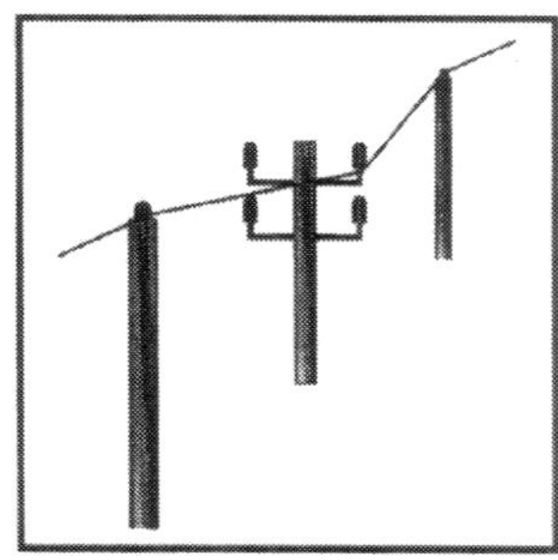

Fig. 18

Rabbi Meir Arik[149] submits that a lenient approach may be in order if the cable is within three *tefachim* of a hypothetical straight line. He explores the possible application here of the halachic mechanism of *"lavud"* (literally: "connected"). halachically, two objects within three *tefachim* of each other are considered connected. Here, we would view the cable as "connected," i.e., repositioned, to its proper hypothetical straight line. Questions, however, may be raised concerning this approach. Rabbi Aryeh Pomeranchek[150] identifies only two classifications of *lavud*, neither of which are applicable to our case. One type of *lavud* allows us to regard any object within

148 *Aruch HaShulchan*, ibid., 362:37. See also *Hilchos Eruvin* 4:2 and note 58. We must note, however, that the *Chazon Ish*, ibid., 71:10 holds that at the moment when an overhead cable that is not taut blows in the wind beyond the width of the *lechayayim* the *eruv* is invalid! We have already noted (Chapter I, note 38) that the *Chazon Ish*, ibid., 111:5 also holds that the overhead "lintel" of a *tzuras ha'pesach* may not be wider than the width of the *lechayayim* that support it. See the discussion on these points in the *Nesivos Shabbos* 19:17,25,42 and notes 39, 94-95. I am indebted to Rabbi Moshe Yitzchok Bernson and Rabbi Elimelech Kornfeld, who pointed out the need to cite these two opinions of the *Chazon Ish*.

149 *Imrei Yosher* 2:133. See also *Yesodei Yeshurun*, ibid., pp. 282-283.

150 *Emek Bracha, Sukkah, siman* 18.

three *tefachim* of another object as if it were connected to that other object; the other type of *lavud* allows us to regard the space between two objects as closed and/or blocked. *Lavud* does not allow us to reposition an object to a place within three *tefachim* of its actual location, which would be necessary to correct this problem.

Often, the upright pole will extend above the crossbar. In such circumstances, even the use of *lavud* would only halachically "reposition" the cable to the side of the pole. We are still not left with a straight line, and may have brought upon ourselves the problem of *tzuras ha'pesach min hatzad.*

Rabbi Ben Zion Sternfeld of Bilsk[151] argues that even a cable veering more than three *tefachim* off the imaginary straight line may be acceptable. Based on this premise it should theoretically be possible to construct an *eruv* around a city with just two *lechayayim.* The cables could encompass the entire city and return to the same *lechayayim* (fig. 19)! Extending this approach to such an absurd conclusion might by itself be sufficient reason to reject such leniency. We may also, however, take issue with the Bilsker Rav's extrapolation from the *Gemara* in *Eruvin* (ibid.). The *Gemara* there discusses the Halacha of *"pischei*

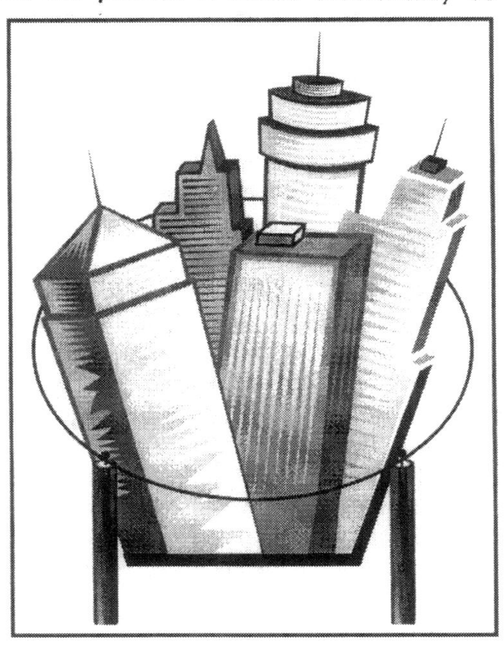

Fig. 19

151 *Sha'arei Zion* 1:3.

shima'ei," door frames whose posts are not straight but consist of stones jutting in and out (fig. 20). The *Gemara* rules that such posts are not true door posts and are therefore not valid *lechayayim*. A *tzuras ha'pesach* with such *lechayayim* is, therefore, invalid.

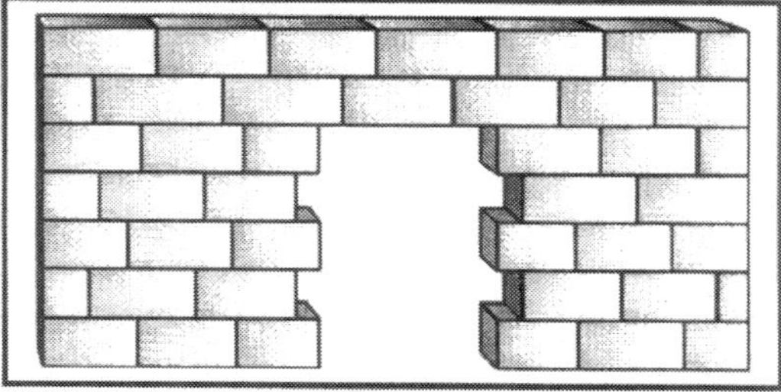

Fig. 20

The Bilsker Rav posits that, since the *Gemara* only discussed and invalidated crooked doorposts, one may deduce that a crooked lintel (in our case, the cable) does not pose a problem. This premise is obviously questionable. The *Gemara* often discusses the most prevalent scenario and leaves us to draw conclusions as to other possible implications. The *Chazon Ish* explicitly invalidates such a *tzuras ha'pesach.*[152] It is worthwhile emphasizing again that any problem can invalidate an entire *eruv*.

4. Problems with the Position of the Pole

Several problems that may arise concern the position of the utility pole and/or the *lechi* attached to the pole. Occasionally the routing of utility cables compels the placement of poles on private property. In and of itself this positioning is not a problem. Often, however, such property is surrounded by fences that the *eruv* must, therefore, cross (fig. 21). The *Mishna Berura*[153] and others rule that such a situation invalidates an *eruv*. Several reasons are given for this ruling. The three most significant are: a) The *lechi* must be recognizable outside the enclosure. (Even if the enclosure is a chain link fence - through which

---

152 Ibid., 71:10. See also *Halachos of the Eruv* Chap. VI, G:2 and note 39; and *Nesivos Shabbos*, ibid., and notes 94-95.

153 363:113. See also *Hilchos Eruvin* 4:19 and note 100.

one can see - the problem is not eliminated. We regard such a fence - because of *lavud* - as a solid wall.) b) The halachic principle of *"beisa k'man d'malia dami"* (literally: a house - or any other ten *tefachim* high enclosure - is regarded as a solid block) requires us to view the entire enclosed area as one solid block.[154] Since the maximum measurement of a *lechi* is four *amos*, if the enclosed area is more than four *amos* on any side, we have a problem.[155] c) The principle of *gud asek* requires us to regard the surrounding fence as if it disrupted the *tzuras ha'pesach*. A similar problem applies in a case where a hedge that is larger than the allowed measurements has grown to surround the *lechi* (fig. 22, see overleaf).[156]

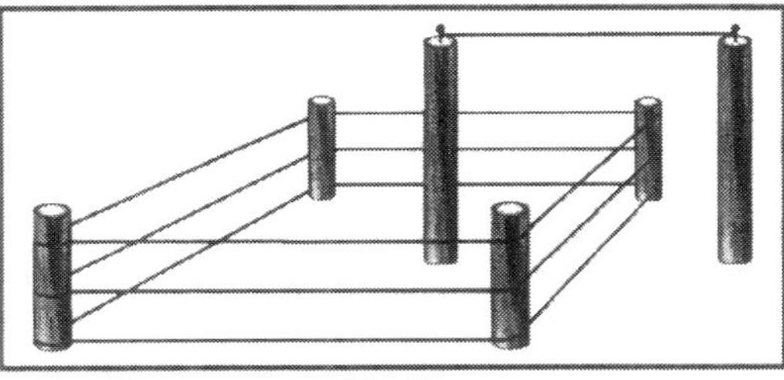

Fig. 21

---

154 *Shabbos* 97a-b. I heard from a certain *Posek* that he is only inclined to be stringent in this area if fences completely surround the pole or *lechi* on all sides, because only then can the principle of *beisa k'man d'malia dami* be applied. From *Rashi*, however, it seems that, in fact, *beisa k'man d'malia dami* only applies to a house, i.e., a structure that is closed on top. Thus, at least from *Rashi*'s perspective, any problem with an enclosed *lechi* would have to be grounded in the other principles that we have noted here.

155 *Eruvin* 5b. See also *Har Tzvi*, ibid., 18:1. There are rare exceptions to this rule. See *Chazon Ish*, ibid., *Eruvin* 70:15-16.

156 See *Nesivos Shabbos* 19:17 note 39. Another relevant case is that of an overhead cable passing through the foliage of a tree. We can view the tree as a *lechi*. Many *Poskim* rule that the cable may pass through a *lechi*. See note 2 above. See, however, *Nesivos Shabbos*, ibid., who notes the concern that over time the branches of the tree may bend the cable away from its correct direct path. See Section 3 above. See also *Hilchos Eruvin* 4:20-25 for an extensive discussion of *tzuros ha'pesach* that pass over structures such as trees, houses and other blockages. Rabbi Tzvi Pesach Frank in *Har Tzvi*, ibid., 18:10 is lenient in cases where the cable runs over or rests on a tree (he does not discuss the case of a cable running through a tree). In this regard, it is noteworthy that the *Nesivos*

The *Avnei Nezer*[157] rebuts the first two problems we have raised. Regarding the first problem, the *Avnei Nezer* states that a *tzuras ha'pesach* need not be recognizable. He proves this from the fact that there is no maximum height above which a *tzuras ha'pesach* is invalid, even though the *Gemara* at the beginning of *Messeches Eruvin* states that the eye does not discern that which is above twenty *amos*.[158] As to the second problem, he says that *beisa k'man d'malia dami* only applies to a covered *reshus ha'yachid*, such as a house. This approach seems borne out by *Rashi*'s explanation of the principle. The *Avnei Nezer* does allow for the third reason. He therefore rules that in such cases the height of the lechi (not the height of the utility pole to which it is attached) must exceed the height of the surrounding fence or hedge by at least ten *tefachim*. We then regard it as a distinct wall above and beyond the surrounding fence whose significance cannot be nullified by an imaginary *gud asek*. Other *Poskim* advance more lenient positions, but even the position of the *Avnei Nezer* is cited by later sources as a leniency to be utilized only under extraordinary conditions (*"heter b'she'as ha'dechak"*).[159] Relying on even more lenient opinions is,

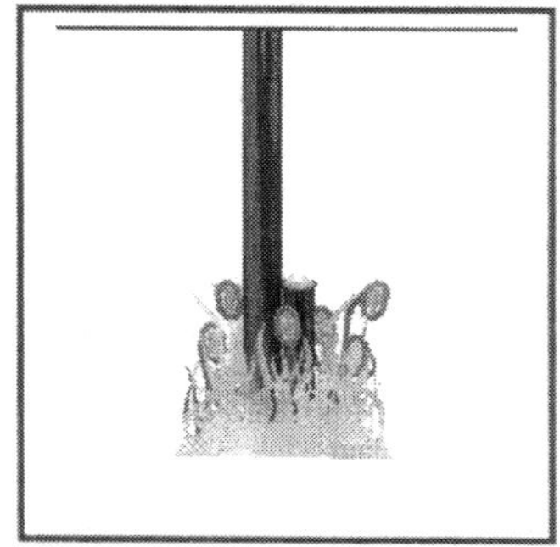

Fig. 22

Shabbos 19:43 note 97 writes that while a wall consisting of shrubbery or hedges constitutes a valid enclosure, it is not clear that an ornamental canopy or gateway cut into the hedge consitutes a valid *tzuras ha'pesach*.

157 Ibid., *siman* 291.

158 *Eruvin* 11a. See, however, *Hilchos Eruvin* 4:3, note 59, and note 140 above for possible exceptions to this rule.

159 *Hilchos Eruvin*, ibid. In note 138 above we noted that it is hard to apply the concept of *she'as ha'dechak* in our day. Rabbi Lange wrote his *sefer* for observant soldiers, who do often face *she'as ha'dechak* situations in the course of duty. Rabbi Lange therefore makes special efforts to identify lenient opinions. Opinions that he feels that one should, if at all possible, not rely upon, should certainly be avoided in constructing an *eruv* for a community facing normal conditions. The

therefore, difficult.

(I once heard in the name of a well-known *Posek* that, in the final analysis, every contemporary *eruv* must rely on some variation of the *Avnei Nezer*'s ruling. He noted that every *tzuras ha'pesach* invariably crosses over parked cars. The cars' dimensions are sufficient to form an interrupting fence. The validity of the *eruv*, therefore, is contingent on our regarding the *eruv* overhead as a distinct wall above and beyond the interrupting fence. An imaginary *gud asek* cannot nullify a wall's significance.)

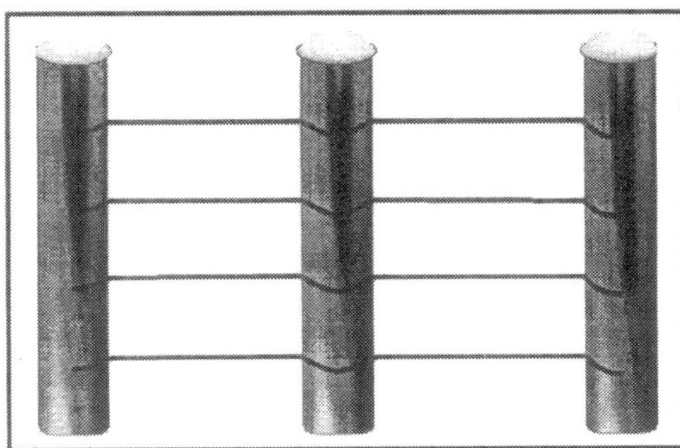

Fig. 23

5. *Fences: A Possible Problem*

Several problems can arise even when an *eruv* makes use of fences. For example: A fence may be constructed of either horizontal rails or strings (fig. 23), or of vertical poles (fig. 24). In such fences, it is important to ascertain that the strings or poles are within three *tefachim* (*lavud*) of each other; that the top string, or the tops of the poles, consistently reach a height of ten *tefachim*; and, that the strings not sway back and forth in prevailing normal

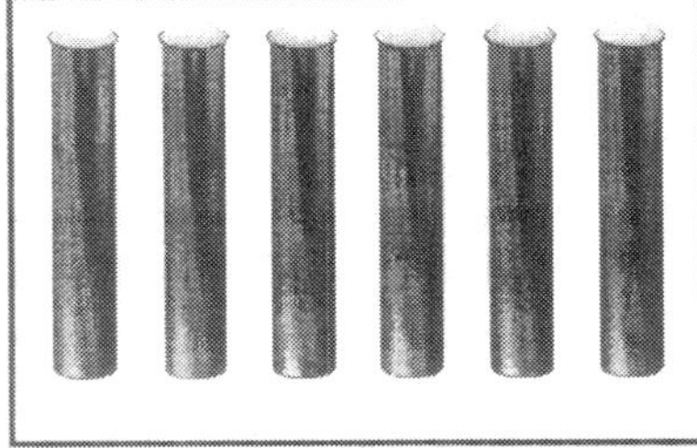

Fig. 24

---

opinion of the *Avnei Nezer* in this regard may be an exception because of the strength of his arguments. The *Chasam Sofer* and other *Poskim* do not require a full ten *tefachim*, but only that the *lechayayim* extend somewhat above the fence or hedge. See *Nesivos Shabbos* 19:19 and notes 43-44.

winds.[160]

Both these fences are considered "poor walls" (*"mechitzos geru'os"*). There are several signifcant limitations on the use of such fences in an *eruv* (including the size of the area they may halachically encompass). They may, however, be used as the fourth wall in an *eruv* that has three true fences (walls, chain-link fences, any other fence with spaces of less than three *tefachim* both horizontally or vertically, or *tzuros ha'pesach*).[161]

6. Transferring from Fence to Cable

Since the use of overhead cable may generate so many problems, it is obviously preferable to use fences and other wall-like structures wherever possible. Another, practical advantage, is that there is far less maintenance involved in a wall-based *eruv*. There are yet other advantages involved in the use of fences and other wall-like structures:

Most importantly, we have seen (in Chapter I, Section 3) that the *Rambam* holds that an *eruv* based exclusively on *tzuros ha'pesach* must have poles spaced no more than ten *amos* apart. We noted there that the *Mishna Berura*[162] advises allowing for the *Rambam's* position. It is therefore preferable that most of the *eruv's* perimeter consist of actual wall-like structures, so that the remainder of the *eruv* may consist of *tzuros ha'pesach* that are broader than ten *amos* even according to the *Rambam's* position.

Another advantage is the extent to which breaks are allowed. In Chapter II, Section 6 we discussed the principle of *omed merubeh al*

---

160 *Shulchan Aruch,* ibid., 362:1-5; *Hilchos Eruvin* 3:1-6.

161 See the parameters in the *Shulchan Aruch*, ibid., 360:1 and the *Bi'ur Halacha* there, *d.h. Kegon Shesi*. There is some question as to whether *omed merubeh al ha'parutz* suffices to establish a fence as a true wall. The prevailing opinion is that it does suffice - see the *Mishna Berura* 360:3 and the *Chazon Ish*, ibid., 77:4.

162 362:59.

ha'parutz k'omed dami that allows us to regard certain breaks or gaps in the wall of a city as if they were closed. The extent to which breaks or gaps are allowed in a *tzuras ha'pesach eruv* is a major problem. Common practice is, therefore, to allow breaks of no more than three *tefachim* between *tzuros ha'pesach*, or between a *tzuras ha'pesach* and a wall-like structure.[163]

A break or gap in a wall has very different parameters.

The most severe scenario of a break in a wall is a gap (*"pirtza"*) at the corner of an enclosure, where, say, the east wall should meet with the north wall. If there is a gap between these walls at the corner (*"pirtza b'keren zavis"*), that gap invalidates the *eruv* - even if it is very small.[164] An unrectified gap that is wider than ten *amos* invalidates an enclosure - even if the rest of the *eruv* is *omed merubeh al ha'parutz*. If a gap that wide exists in an *eruv*, it must be rectified by a *tzuras ha'pesach*.[165] A gap that is narrower than ten *amos* may also

---

163 See *Nesivos Shabbos* 14:15, note 33 and 19:16, note 37. The *Nesivos Shabbos* in the latter note quotes the *Biur Halacha* 363:6 *d.h. Tzarich* who advises stringency in this matter. The *Nesivos Shabbos* infers from this that *b'she'as ha'dechak* one may be lenient (see note 138 above).

164 *Shulchan Aruch*, ibid., 361:2. The *Chazon Ish*, ibid., 72:1, holds that a *pirtza b'keren zavis* invalidates a *reshus ha'yachid me'd'oraysa*. The *Mishna Berura* there, 361:9, rules that since such a gap invalidates the enclosure because we cannot regard it as an opening (since openings are not made at corners - *"pirtza b'keren zavis lo avid inshei"*), if one identified it as a legitimate opening in a wall by building a *tzuras ha'pesach* there, the enclosure is then valid. The *Minchas Yitzchak* 6:34 says that it is sufficient to build a door, even without a *tzuras ha'pesach*. This is in line with his opinion concerning *delasos*, see below, note 202.

There is some disagreement over what minimum width of the gap at the corner invalidates the enclosure. See, also, *Nesivos Shabbos* 14:4, note 8, where he also discusses the status of a round enclosure.

165 *Shulchan Aruch*, ibid., 362:9. See the *Mishna Berura* there, 362:52. The *Chazon Ish* that we discussed at length in Chapter III, Section 6 (*Orach Chaim* 107:5) holds that *me'd'oraysa, omed merubeh al ha'parutz* overrides a gap even if it is greater than ten *amos*. The *Igros Moshe*, ibid., 5:28:3 rejects this *Chazon Ish*, and holds that the breaks of more than ten *amos* invalidate the enclosure even *me'd'oraysa* (if they are not rectified by *tzuras ha'pesach*). Reb Moshe's reasoning here is unclear. See the attempt by the editors of this, the latest volume of the *Igros Moshe*, there to clarify the issue. See also above, Chapter III, note 134.

invalidate an enclosure - if it takes up an entire side (i.e., direction, north, south, east or west) of the *eruv* - unless the gap is on the fourth side of the *eruv*, in which case, as we have seen (Chapter I, Section 3), posts or beams suffice.[166]

A gap that is less than ten *amos* wide can also invalidate an enclosure even if it does not take up an entire side - if there is more open space than wall-like structure on that side of the *eruv*.[167]

If a gap in a walled enclosure (one that is at least *omed k'parutz*) is less than ten *amos* (but more than four *tefachim*) wide, then its status depends on whether it is used as a pathway or thoroughfare. If used as a thoroughfare, a post or beam (if it is defined as a *mavoi*; two posts, if it is defined as a courtyard) must be fixed to the adjacent wall where the thoroughfare exits the enclosure (see Chapter I, Section 3). Since current practice is to impart to all our enclosures the status of courtyards, two posts, one affixed to each side of the thoroughfare,

---

166 *Shulchan Aruch*, ibid., 363:1. See also *Bi'ur Halacha* 362:8, *d.h. Parutz Merubeh* and *Nesivos Shabbos* 14:6 and note 13.

167 *Shulchan Aruch*, ibid., 362:8-9. The *Maharal, Eruvin* 11a, and others suggest that we determine *omed merubeh* on the basis of the entire perimeter. Since the *Shulchan Aruch* rules there that *omed k'parutz* is sufficient, if the entire enclosure was at least 50% wall-like structure, then gaps of up to ten *amos* anywhere along the perimeter would not invalidate the *eruv*. The *Mishna Berura* 362:45, however, rules that we must also take each side independently. Thus, the side in which the gap exists must in and of itself be *omed k'parutz* in order to allow a gap of less than ten *amos* without any additional rectification. As we have mentioned, there are many *Poskim* that do not take *tzuros ha'pesach* into account in making this determination (see *Nesivos Shabbos* 14:15 and note 33). Thus, to allow breaks of up to ten *amos* would require actual wall-like structure over at least 50% of the entire perimeter of the *eruv*, and over the length of each side of the *eruv* as well. See *Nesivos Shabbos* 14:7-16 for more details on how to reckon the *omed* vs. the *parutz*.

(It seems that these parameters of *omed k'parutz* are more stringent than those required to fulfill the *Rambam*'s criterion that there be more wall-like structure than *tzuras ha'pesach* to allow the *tzuros ha'pesach* to be more than ten *amos* wide that we discussed in Chapter I, section 3. It appears that there is no need, vis-à-vis the *Rambam*'s opinion, to assess each side independently, and it suffices to have *omed k'parutz* taking the entire perimeter into account.)

are necessary.[168]

---

168 *Shulchan Aruch*, ibid., 363:26. See *Nesivos Shabbos* 20:15 and note 34.

We should note a difficult *Sha'ar Ha'Tziyun* in this regard. The *Noda B'Yehuda, Mahadura Tinyana, siman* 42 (that we cited previously in Chapter I, note 56) writes to a former student, questioning his city's *eruv*:

> Concerning your question, that although your city is completely open on its fourth side, there is a river running there, and that there are ten *tefachim* [of a riverbank] above the water, but that there is a bridge there [across the river] that is more than ten *amos* wide. And you wanted to permit [carrying in the city without any further rectification] based on the *Tosafos Shabbos* 363:6, who states that a bridge does not automatically override any wall underneath it. Rather, a bridge overrides the wall underneath it is because masses walk on it, and masses negate walls [*asu rabbim u'mevatlei mechitzta*] only where the wall below is not artificial but natural. And you also derived from the *Tosafos Shabbos*, relying on the *Magen Avraham* 363:40 as well, that the quantity that constitute "masses" that negate a wall is 600,000. You also relied on the *Terumas Ha'Deshen, siman* 74, that one should not cast aspersions on leniencies of prior generations.
>
> You should know that I do not agree with your lenient approach. Were the *Tosafos Shabbos* to have held as you say, it would have been incumbent upon him to clarify from where he derived that a bridge does not invalidate an *eruv* because it is considered a break [*pirtza*], but because of the masses that pass and make use of it. In my opinion, the *Tosafos Shabbos* did not mean this. Rather, his intent in saying: "And this is also the rule when there is a bridge as well," is to refer to the ruling of the *Magen Avraham* who invalidates an *eruv* if boats ride over it on their way to port. Referring to this, the *Tosafos Shabbos* writes that this is also true about a bridge - because it is a *pirtza*...

The *Noda B'Yehuda* then goes on to bring three proofs that a bridge is a bona fide *pirtza* that requires rectification (even if it is used by relatively few people, or crosses over artificial walls, so that no problem of *asu rabbim* exists) - since it is a pathway or thoroughfare. He dismisses his student's application of the *Terumas Ha'Deshen*, stating that it is only relevant where the former leniency was halachically sound, as opposed to the case under discussion, where the former leniency was simply a mistake. The *Noda B'Yehuda* concludes that it is necessary, in this case, to construct a *tzuras ha'pesach*.

The *Sha'ar Ha'Tziyun* 363:95, cites the *Noda B'Yehuda*. He writes that although others ruled that a bridge that is less than ten *amos* wide needs no rectification, it is evident from the *Noda B'Yehuda* that even a bridge that is less than ten *amos* wide does require a "rectification" ["*tikkun*"]. The *Chazon Ish*, ibid., 65:60, assumes that the *Sha'ar Ha'Tziyun* meant to mandate a *tzuras ha'pesach*, and rejects that position, stating that as a *pirtza* or *pesach* of less than ten *amos*, only one post four *tefachim* wide, or two posts, each a "*mashehu*" wide, would be

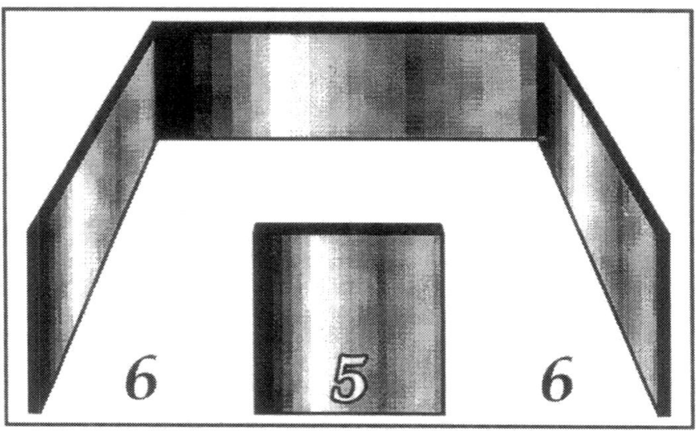

Fig. 25

If the gap in a wall or fence is not used as a pathway or thoroughfare, and is less than ten *amos* wide, then we require no rectification (- if there is no opening on the other side of the enclosure directly across from the one in question).[169]

---

necessary. Perhaps we might propose that the *Sha'ar Ha'Tziyun* also agrees with this opinion - after all, the *Noda B'Yehuda* certainly was not discussing a bridge narrower than ten *amos* when he required a *tzuras ha'pesach*. Rather, the *Sha'ar Ha'Tziyun* only meant to say that since the *Noda B'Yehuda* established that a bridge is inherently a *pirtza* (as opposed to his student's understanding that it only created the extrinsic problem of *asu rabbim*), even where that opening is less than ten *tefachim*, a rectification is necessary - but not necessarily that of *tzuras ha'pesach*, rather, even that of posts.

169 See the *Nesivos Shabbos* 20:14-15 and notes 30-34.

It is important to note the rule of *"asi avira d'hay gisa u'd'hay gisa u'mevatel lei"* (*Eruvin* 10b; *Shulchan Aruch*, ibid., 363:34). This principle translates as: "The open space on both sides [of the structure] comes and cancels it." The simplest application of this principle is a case where on one side of a walled enclosure there is an open space of, say, six *amos*, then a standing structure of five *amos*, then again an open space of six *amos* (fig. 25). In this case, the five *amos* long structure is negated by the surrounding open space and the open spaces combine to create a *pirtza* of more than seventeen *amos*. This principle applies even if the open space on one side is equal in length to the structure, as long as the space on the other side is somewhat longer. There are many complex variations of this problem, especially when an *eruv* has a series of contiguous structures and open spaces. See the details in *Hilchos Shabbos* 6:3-7 and *Nesivos Shabbos* 14:7.

Usually, however, it is difficult to rely on fences alone. In most municipal *eruvin*, it is difficult, if not impossible, even to secure the advantage of *omed merubeh al ha'parutz* or *omed k'parutz*. Even in an ideal scenario, fences are inevitably interrupted to allow streets to pass through. Since these streets are usually wider than ten *amos*, *tzuros ha'pesach* must be constructed to link the fence on one side of the street to its continuation on the other side. Instead of building a new *tzuras ha'pesach* across the street, it is often more expedient to "jump" to an overhead cable that crosses the street.[170]

The latter option frequently raises a problem. Even in the best of circumstances, i.e., where the overhead cables are directly over the utility pole, the poles are usually behind and not within three *tefachim* of the fence (fig. 26). That the poles are behind the fence returns us to the previous problem of *lechayayim* enclosed by fences (see above, Section 4). That the poles are more than three *tefachim* away from the fence raises an additional problem: What connects the fence to the overhead cable? The fence is usually larger than the allowable measurements for a

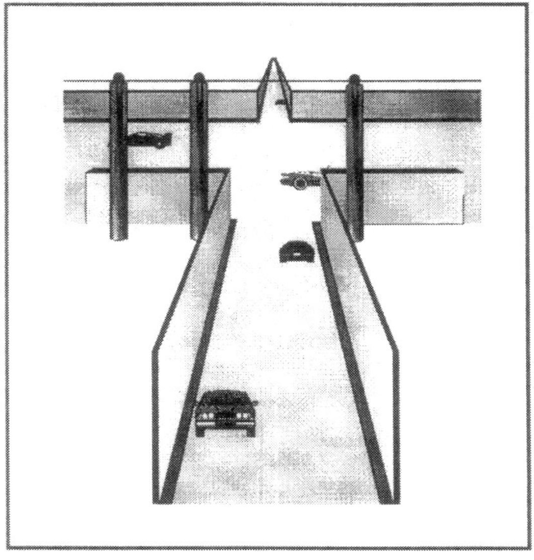

Fig. 26

[170] Insuring an uninterrupted line is a little tricky when riverbanks used as *mechitzos* are interrupted by bridges. The *lechayayim* of the *tzuras ha'pesach* used to cross the bridge must be within three *tefachim* of the banks' usable *tel hamislaket*. See *Nesivos Shabbos* 19:16, note 36.

lechi, so drawing the *gud asek* line up from the fence does not help. If the poles were within three *tefachim* of the fence we could probably use *lavud* to validate the *eruv*.[171] In the case we have described, however, we have to turn to the *Chazon Ish* for guidance.[172]

The *Chazon Ish* discusses a case where structures used in constructing an enclosure connect or overlap, but do not meet (fig. 27). In the *Chazon Ish*'s case, a north-south wall or *tzuras ha'pesach*

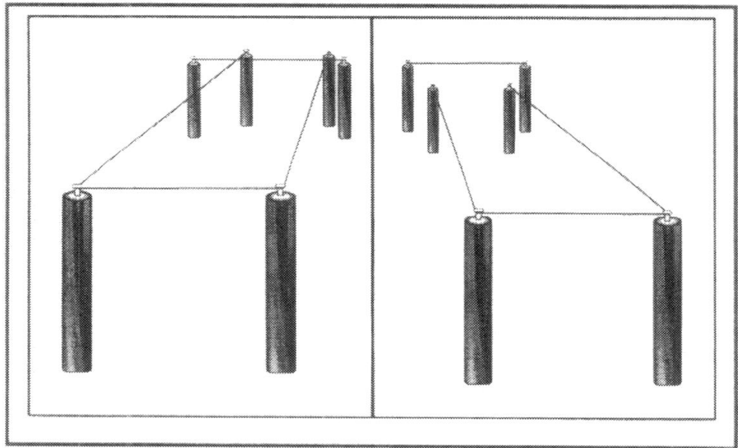

Fig. 27

---

171 See *Halachos of the Eruv* Chap. VII, A:1-2. Even, however, were one to be satisfied with a *she'as ha'dechak eruv* (see note 138 above) of the sort mentioned in note 159 above, this principle could not apply to the case in question here. The principle of *omed merubeh* used to allow breaks of less than ten *amos* applies only to cases where the two structures of *omed merubeh* are in line and do not overlap. Here, the two structures have overlapped and crossed over each other. They must now double back, so to speak, and meet each other (fig. 27, left-hand side). This is not a case of *omed merubeh* crossing and closing a gap. This is a case where thereis no gap, thus by definition eliminating any application of *omed merubeh al ha'parutz*. Here we must connect two structures, which must therefore be within *lavud* of each other.

172 Ibid., 70:21. See also *Kehillos Ya'akov, Eruvin, siman* 6; *Hilchos Eruvin* 4:21; and, *Nesivos Shabbos* 19:18 and note 42.

bisects an east-west *tzuras ha'pesach*, or connects with it at points between the east-west's *tzuras ha'pesach*'s lechayayim.[173] The north-south wall or *tzuras ha'pesach* halachically eliminates the *lechayayim* of the east-west *tzuras ha'pesach*. Since they are beyond the area of the enclosure, they are halachically insignificant. We may apply the same ruling to our case. To validate this enclosure a *lechi* would have to be placed on the outside of the fence directly underneath the overhead cable (thus creating a *gud asek*).

7. *Utilizing Other Structures: Natural Walls*

Let us now discuss problems that arise when such structures are used in constructing an *eruv*. It is preferable to use man-made walls. Natural walls, such as cliffs and riverbanks, are considered halachically valid. Most *Poskim*,[174] however, hold that such walls are *"einam mukafim l'dira"* (literally: not surrounding for dwelling).[175] They were not made with the intent to sustain habitation, and they therefore cannot enclose an area that is larger than five thousand square *amos* (a *"beis se'asayim"*). This limitation, however, precludes only an *eruv* consisting <u>entirely</u> of natural walls, such as an island surrounded by cliffs. If, however, a section - at least ten *amos* long - of such an *eruv* consists of an artificial structure such as a fence or *tzuras ha'pesach*, that section allows us to consider the entire perimeter as properly *mukaf l'dira* (surrounded for dwelling).[176]

173 This is even true where the *tzuras ha'pesach* is not actually bisected, as long as the *lechayayim* are outside the area of the enclosure (fig. 28). We have discussed fences and structures that bisect *tzuros ha'pesach*. The *Chazon Ish*, ibid., 70:19 notes that structures that run parallel and within four *tefachim* of a *tzuras ha'pesach* may invalidate the *eruv*. If these structures are <u>outside</u> the area enclosed by the *eruv* they do not present a problem. If, however, they are inside that area, then the character of the "doorway" is negated - because it opens into too small an area to be considered an "enclosed area." See *Hilchos Eruvin* 4:25 for an extensive discussion of the parameters of such blockages.

174 *Shulchan Aruch*, ibid., 358:3; *Hilchos Eruvin* 3:7-12, 7:1-2.

175 *Shulchan Aruch*, ibid., 358:1.

176 I am indebted to Rabbi Moshe Yitzchok Bernson and Rabbi Akiva Yosef Kaplan

(Another drawback that natural walls present is that they are subject to the problem of *asu rabbim u'mevatlei mechitzta* that we have dealt with above in Chapter I, Sections 2, 4 and 5, and Chapter II, Section 6.[177])

The major problem involved in the use of riverbanks or hillsides in the perimeter of an *eruv* is encountered in the question of their sheerness. A perpendicular bank or cliff is certainly a valid wall. Most riverbanks or hillsides, however, rise in a gradual slope. How gradual a slope may be considered a valid wall?

The *Gemara* defines the acceptable gradient as a *"tel hamislaket asara mitoch arba,"* a slope that rises ten *tefachim* within the distance of four *amos*.[178] According to most *Poskim* we measure the four *amos* along the actual slope, so when we depict the slope as a right triangle (fig. 28), the hypotenuse is four *amos* (twenty-four *tefachim*) long, and

---

for noting that the previous editions incorrectly stated the Halacha (too stringently!) in this case. The correction is based on the *Shulchan Aruch*, ibid., 358:2. See, however, the next note.

177 In the famous *teshuva* in *Achi'ezer* 4:8 concerning Paris Rabbi Chaim Ozer Grodziensky makes clear that the entire perimeter of natural walls must be bolstered by artificial walls to consider it a valid enclosure, unless there exists the mitigating factor we mentioned above, in Chapter II, Section 4 and note 63, i.e., that the walls only encompass an area that is sufficiently compact that one could see all the walls surrounding the area. Reb Chaim Ozer, however, defines that parameter slightly differently: "Any area that people would normally enclose is defined as [allowing an individual] to recognize that he is within walls, even if these walls are natural walls." He cites the *Chazon Ish*, ibid., 107:1, who learns that this is the meaning of the *Tosafos, Eruvin* 22b, *d.h. Eeleima*. He notes that since Paris once possessed walls that were as extensive as the proposed *eruv*, they clearly fulfill that parameter. We should stress, however, that since Reb Chaim Ozer's opinion was that Paris encompasses areas defined as *reshuyos ha'rabbim*, he was loathe to rely on this factor by itself, and also took the phenomenon of artificial bolstering into account in formulating his lenient ruling.

Thus, while the rectification of ten *amos* along a perimeter of natural walls will allow the enclosed area to be considered *mukaf l'dira*, it does not eliminate the problem of *asu rabbim u'mevatlei mechitzta*, for which other halachic solutions (that we have discussed previously) must be identified.

178 *Shabbos* 100a.

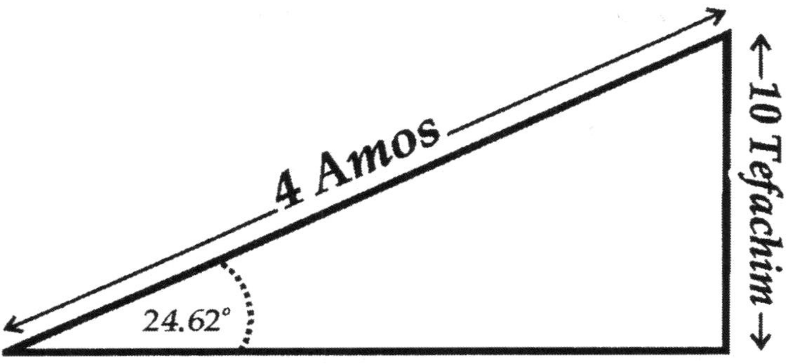

Fig. 28

the side is ten *tefachim* high.[179] Following the computations through, the base of the triangle would be 21.8 *tefachim* long, and the angle of the slope would be 24.62°.[180] A slope of this gradient is quite steep. One may mistakenly perceive or assume that a specific riverbank or hillside meets these criteria, when in reality it does not. It is, therefore, imperative that expert, objective surveyors be employed to verify that the slope is in fact sufficiently steep to comprise a *tel hamislaket*.

It is unclear how often the slope must be surveyed. Riverbanks and hillsides are obviously susceptible to natural erosion and artificial alteration. Professional surveys are extended and expensive projects. It is thus impractical to survey slopes weekly. The parameters of various *eruvin* are liable to differ significantly. The hillsides and riverbanks in some *eruvin* may tend to remain stable over long periods of time, while in other *eruvin* they may be subject to frequent natural and artificial forces that are liable to diminish their gradients. It seems that the *Rav Ha'Machshir* (certifying rabbinic authority) of an *eruv* must set specific guidelines for every *eruv* differently, based on the specific situation in that place at that time.[181]

---

179 See *Nesivos Shabbos* 16:6 and note 18.

180 Ibid., p. 186; *Hilchos Eruvin* 1:1 and note 4.

181 It is customary to inspect municipal *eruvin* weekly. See *Yesodei Yeshurun*, ibid., pp. 331-332 for a discussion of the sources upon which the custom is based. I am

We must note that there are several complications that are uniquely relevant to the use of *tel hamislaket*. For example, since the terrain of a hillside or riverbank generally does not climb in a continuous slope, it is essential to insure that the proper dimensions and proportions of a *tel hamislaket* are maintained in at least some section of the embankment, and that the *tel hamislaket* continues unbroken along the entire embankment.[182] As with all other facets of *eruv* construction, a competent rabbinic authority must be brought for on-site inspections of the terrain.

8. Utilizing Other Structures: Elevated Train Tracks and Highway Viaducts

Another prevalent issue concerning wall-like structures is perhaps best explored through further examination of the history of *eruvin* in New York City (see above, Chapter II, Section 5).

As we have already mentioned, the Sherpser Rav formulated his position based on the following scenario: The Lower East Side was surrounded on three sides by the walls that front on the East River, and on the fourth side by the Third Avenue elevated train line (fig. 9). An elevated train line may look just like a classic *tzuras ha'pesach*:

---

indebted to Rabbi Ari Zivotofsky for the information that there are some communities that are very stringent when it comes to this inspection, to the extent that when *Yom Tov* falls on a Friday and precludes an effective inspection, these communities will not rely on an inspection conducted on Wednesday or Thursday before *Yom Tov*, and will assume the *eruv* to be invalid for the following *Shabbos*. Thus, the parameters of inspections are very subjective, and it is not necessarily possible to extrapolate from the guidelines of a community with an *eruv* that is subject to frequent manipulation by utility companies, etc., to a community with an *eruv* that is rarely disturbed, and vice versa.

182 There are cases in which breaks of up to three *tefachim* in the height of a slope vertically and breaks of up to ten *amos* in the continuity of the slope horizontally are permitted. The parameters of this case and several other scenarios involving *tel hamislaket* are complex. See *Nesivos Shabbos* 16:7-14.

We may see the support beams as *lechayayim* and the overhead train tracks as the lintel. The *She'arim Mitzuyanim B'Halacha* quotes such an approach in the name of the *Even Yekara.*[183] The *She'arim Mitzuyanim B'Halacha* himself, however, based on a *Magen Avraham,*[184] takes issue with the *Even Yekara.* A door frame is distinct from the walls and ceiling of the room to which it is affixed. Logic then dictates that the door frame effect that forms a *tzuras ha'pesach* also requires that the *lechayayim* and lintel be distinct from the walls of the structure to which they are affixed.[185] The *She'arim Mitzuyanim*

---

183 See the *She'arim Mitzuyanim B'Halacha* 82:9 and the *Kuntres Acharon* there.

184 363:28. The *Magen Avraham* there states that the walls that surround three sides of an alley (a *"mavoi"*) cannot be considered the *lechayayim* for a *tzuras ha'pesach* on the courtyard's fourth side. The *Magen Avraham* does not explain the rationale for his ruling (see *Nesivos Shabbos* 19:17, note 39). A possible interpretation of the *Magen Avraham's* position is that *lechayayim* cannot exceed a certain maximum *shiur* (measurement). See the *Chazon Ish*, ibid., 70:16. (This *Chazon Ish* is discussed at length in *Hilchos Eruvin* 4:12 and notes 77-78, but one may differ with Rabbi Lange's interpretation of the *Chazon Ish*'s cases.) The *Chazon Ish* there raises the possibility that in certain cases the maximum *shiur* is three or four *tefachim*. Under normal circumstances, however, it seems that the maximum *shiur* is four *amos*. See *Nesivos Shabbos*, ibid., note 40, in the name of the *Makor Chaim*. Structures that long are no longer viewed as the "door posts" *(lechayayim)* of a "door frame" *(tzuras ha'pesach)* - they are walls. Elevated train line embankments or overpasses that are more than four *amos* long would therefore not be halachically suitable to serve as *lechayayim*. The *Chelkas Ya'akov* 1:166.4 presents arguments that would allow the use of "long" *lechayayim* such as embankments that support elevated train lines. Some rabbinic authorities follow the *Chelkas Ya'akov*'s ruling in this area. The *Chelkas Ya'akov*'s reasoning and proofs, however, are controversial and difficult to follow, and seem not to be in accordance with the opinions of the *Poskim* mentioned previously in this paragraph. See also *Nesivos Shabbos* 19:17 and note 39.

The *Nesivos Shabbos* there is unsure as to the status of a valid (ten *tefachim* high) sidepost situated atop a wall (he recognizes a possible dichotomy between a case where the wall itself is ten *tefachim* high and where it is lower than that measurement). Rabbi Lange, *Hilchos Eruvin* 4:23, is inclined to leniency, but then casts doubt on his own position in note 105. A related issue is the question whether it is permitted to place a *tzuras ha'pesach* on or across hillsides or riverbanks that rise at steep enough angles to be considered walls - see *Nesivos Shabbos* there 19:23 and notes 48-49.

185 See the *Chazon Ish*, ibid., 70:17 and the interpretation thereof in *Hilchos Eruvin*, 4:12, note 79. Rabbi Lange understands that the *Chazon Ish* forbids the case

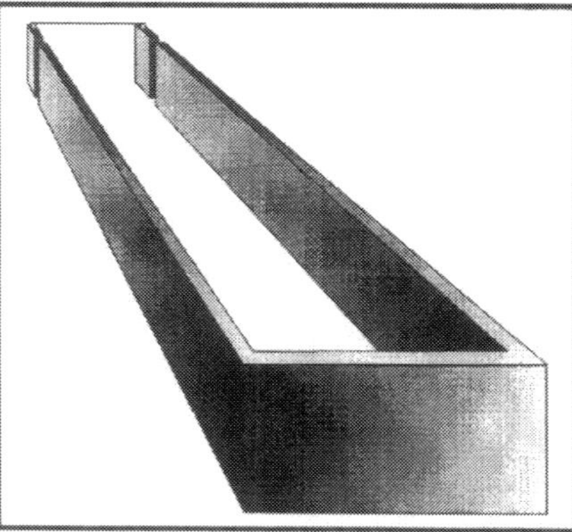

Fig. 29

pictured in fig. 29. (If the *tzuras ha'pesach* is contiguous - within three *tefachim* - to the walls; if, however, the *tzuras ha'pesach* is next to another *tzuras ha'pesach*, he notes that even the *Chazon Ish* would rule leniently.) It seems, however, that the interpretation is incorrect. The *Chazon Ish* holds that a *tzuras ha'pesach* must be distinct and recognizable to those who stand within the area that the *tzuras ha'pesach* encloses. Consequently, the *Chazon Ish* - ibid., and, 67:23, 70:16, 74:12, 86:4-5; and, *Yoreh De'ah* 172:2 - states that *lechayayim* of a *tzuras ha'pesach* may not be placed behind the walls of a *mavoi*, nor even affixed to their outermost edge (fig. 30). He proves this from a *Gemara* in *Eruvin*

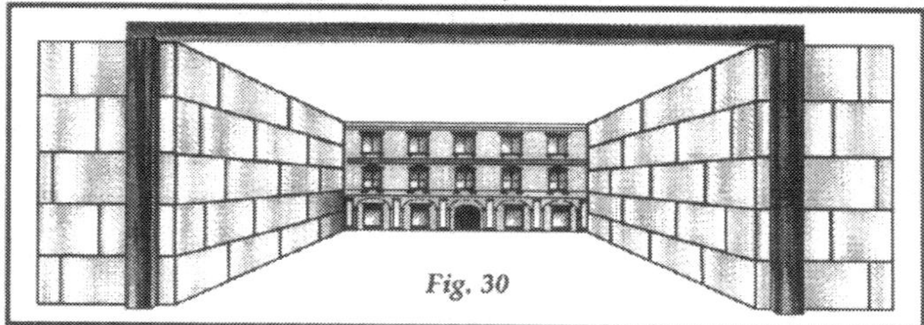

Fig. 30

24b (see his discussion there, in *Yoreh De'ah* 86:4-5). He also invalidates *lechayayim* that - from the perspective of one standing within the *mavoi* - are flush and indistinct from the wall to which they are attached (fig. 31). The *Nesivos Shabbos* 19:18 and notes 41-42 has difficulties with the *Chazon Ish*, and regards his rulings in this matter as only sufficient to create a "*safek*" (a doubtful case) - of course, a *safek* that we derive from a *Chazon Ish* is not insignificant! He also describes cases in which the *Chazon Ish* would allow such *lechayayim*. In any event, it seems evident that the case as drawn in fig. 29 would not constitue a problem, as the *lechayayim* therein are certainly distinct and recognizable. The *Nesivos Shabbos* also notes that the *Chazon Ish*'s stringent position only pertains to the sideposts, but not to the "lintel" - the cable or string overhead. See also *Nesivos Shabbos* 19:22 and note 46.

B'Halacha rules, therefore, that we may only regard a bridge or overpass as a *tzuras ha'pesach* if it has features that we may regard as distinct from its wall. The *Chazon Ish* rules this way as well.[186]

It is possible that another principle may prevent us from viewing an elevated train line, bridge, highway overpass, or toll booth as a *tzuras ha'pesach*. In 1952, Rabbi Raphael Ber Weissmandel wrote a proposal to permit carrying on *Shabbos* in Brooklyn on the basis of the elevated train lines. His rationale, however, was not based on the

---

186 The *Chazon Ish, Orach Chaim,* 111:5 derives this ruling from the *Magen Avraham* cited in note 184. The *Chazon Ish* there discusses several basic issues in *Hilchos Eruvin*. These include why we do not place *mezuzos* on a *tzuras ha'pesach* and why utility poles that were not constructed for an *eruv* may later be used to create one without any tangible rectifications. The *Chazon Ish* there also advances a significant leniency. He allows distinct features of an overpass or structure (such as support girders and beams) to be used as part of a *tzuras ha'pesach* even if they were originally constructed *"le'achzukai tikra"* - to support the roof - which is problematic in *Hilchos Mezuza* (see, however, above, note 148). He proves this from the *sugya* of *pischei shima'ei*, from the *Biur HaGr"a, Orach Chaim* 630:2 and other sources. I am indebted to Rabbi Shlomo Miller and Rabbi Elimelech Kornfeld for directing me to this *Chazon Ish*.

(The *Nesivos Shabbos*, 19:17 note 39 (at the very end) does not allow the use of *gud asek* in such scenarios, i.e., requiring that the *lechi* extend all the way up to the girder or other feature in use as the "lintel." He bases this position on the *Chazon Ish, Yoreh De'ah* 172:2. I do not understand how the *Nesivos Shabbos* derived this stringency from that *Chazon Ish*, as the *Chazon Ish* there is discussing a *sukka* and the use of its *schach* as a "lintel." The cases are not similar. The *Chazon Ish* there requires the door posts to reach all the way up to the *schach* because the *schach* has no distinct features over the door posts and is therefore deficient - in contradistinction to the distinct features under discussion here.)

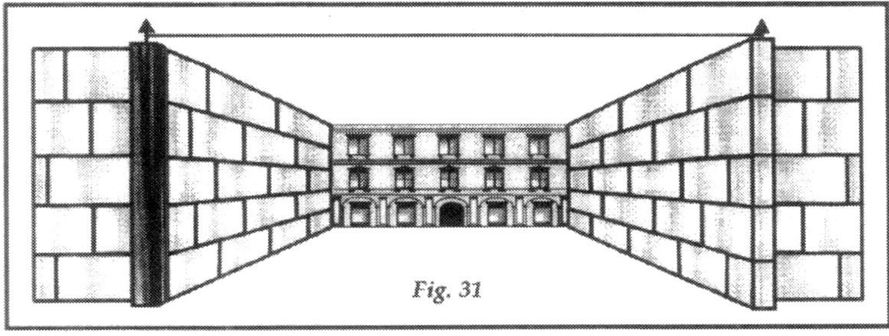

Fig. 31

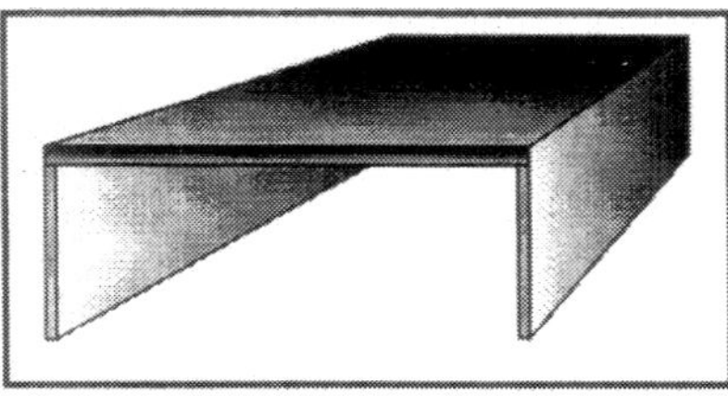

Fig. 32

principle of *tzuras ha'pesach*, but on that of *"pi tikra yored v'sosem"* (literally: the lip of a roof comes down and closes)[187] (fig. 32). The principle, as defined in the *Shulchan Aruch*, is that, when a roof is at least four *tefachim* by four *tefachim* and set atop two complete walls, we view the thickness of the roof as an imaginary wall for the remaining two sides.[188] Rabbi Moshe Feinstein disagreed with Rabbi Weissmandel's application of this principle to elevated train lines.[189] Among his reasons was his observation that several *Rishonim* do not view the principle of *pi tikra* as creating walls, but as creating a defined area (underneath the ceiling) in which one is allowed to carry. Thus, perhaps one might be permitted to carry directly underneath the elevated tracks, but the tracks could still not serve to enclose the area that they enclose.

It seems significant that neither Rabbi Weissmandel nor Reb Moshe discussed the possibility that the elevated train line might serve as a *tzuras ha'pesach*. We may assume that the reason for this omission is related to the logic we developed above, that a *tzuras*

---

187 *Eruvin* 94b. In the *Tikvas Zecharia*, Rabbi Rosenfeld notes that telegraph poles often support a thicket of wires at their tops. These wires are well within three *tefachim* of each other. Viewing them, halachically, as connected, allows one to consider the thicket as a roof. One could then apply the principle of *pi tikra yored v'sosem* to them. In practice, however, Rabbi Rosenfeld does not utilize this approach in sanctioning the use of the telegraph poles and wires as halachic walls, preferring instead the already accepted trend to view them as comprising *tzuros ha'pesach*. He does, however, propose that the presence of these "roofs" along the length of a street will diminish their potential to be regarded as a *reshus ha'rabbim*, since roofed over *reshuyos ha'rabbim* are automatically downgraded to *carmelis* status. - see *Nesivos Shabbos* 3:1 and note 6, where he considers (inconclusively) how much of a roof is necessary to negate a *reshus ha'rabbim*.

188 *Shulchan Aruch,Orach Chaim*, 361:2.

189 *Igros Moshe*, ibid., 1:138.

ha'pesach must resemble a traditional door frame. By definition, a *tzuras ha'pesach* whose lintel is more than four *tefâchim* wide is a roof. We can no longer view it as a door frame.[190]

Fig. 33

190 One of my *Rabbeim* brought evidence that a roof cannot serve as *tzuras ha'pesach* from an observation that in *Eruvin* 94b Rav and Shmuel argue whether the roof of an *achsadra* (a shelter consisting of a roof supported by poles and no more than two walls) allows one to carry beneath it on *Shabbos* because of *pi tikra yored v'sosem* or not. Neither *Amora* entertains the seemingly obvious possibility of *tzuras ha'pesach*. The *Chazon Ish* cited above in note 186 brings this proof as well. As we have mentioned, the *Nesivos Shabbos* 19:17, end of note 39, discusses the possibility of using an overhang or ridge on a roof (fig. 33) as the lintel of a *tzuras ha'pesach*. He reasons that this is permissible where such a feature - and accompanying *lechayayim* - are at the edge of the roof. This would apply to an overhang on an overpass or elevated train line. Where the overhang is at the edge of the overpass it may be incorporated in an *eruv*. Cases where only a *lechi* is under the extension of a roof are problematic. See *Halachos of the Eruv* Chap. VII, J and note 20. The edge of the overhang may be considered a *pi tikra*, effectively cutting off the *lechi* from the rest of the *eruv* (fig. 34, see overleaf).

9. The "Disappearing" Halacha of Karpeifos

Several years ago, during a routine tour of an *eruv* located in a coastal community, it was discovered that the *eruv* encompassed a large saltwater inlet. This inlet had previously gone unnoticed because a thicket of reeds surrounded it. Examination of other thickets in the area revealed that some of them were in reality marshes. These proved impassable, even by local youth equipped with machetes for the specific purpose of trying to traverse these thickets! The problem that had arisen was the obscure Halacha of *"karpaf."*

We have already mentioned the problem of natural walls that are *einam mukafim l'dira*. An area may also be considered *eino mukaf l'dira* if it is not an area designated for human habitation. We call such an area a *karpaf*. If a *karpaf* that is larger than five thousand square *amos* (a *"beis se'asayim"*) is included within an *eruv* it renders the <u>entire</u> *eruv* invalid.[191] The *Poskim* extend the definition of human habitation to include any use of the area in question for human needs. This would include parks and any other area suitable for walking or

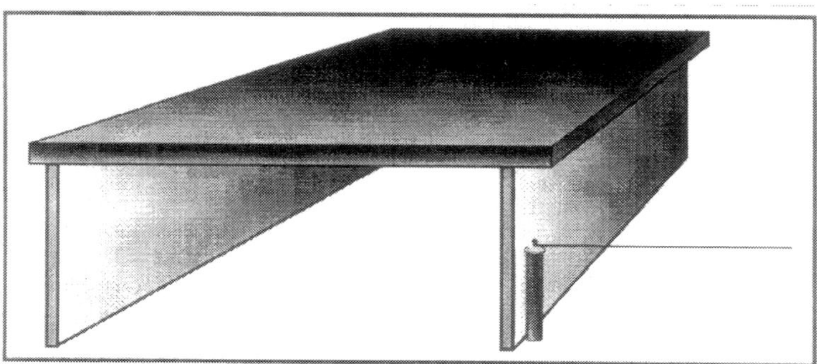

Fig. 34

191 *Shulchan Aruch*, 358:9. See also *Hilchos Eruvin* 7:3-15; *Yesodei Yeshurun*, ibid., pp. 261-265; *She'arim Metzuyanim B'Halacha* 83:4-6 and the *Kuntres Acharon* there; *Tzitz Eliezer* 13:41; and *Nesivos Shabbos* 12-13. The Halachos of *karpaf* are amazingly complex. Many *Acharonim* have written *teshuvos* on the subject, and their *teshuvos* are frequently contradictory, as they often vehemently disagree with each other in deciding practical Halacha. A succinct summary of the various methodologies brought to bear in permitting *karpeifos* within an *eruv* can be found in Rabbi Kroizer's essay, *No'am*, vol. 1, pp. 230-233.

strolling, but not planted fields, unless there are walking paths between the furrows.[192] The *Rashba*, quoted by the *Shulchan Aruch*, rules that if a body of water included within an *eruv* is suitable for human consumption or use, even if its water is suitable only for laundry, it does not invalidate the *eruv* - even if it is larger than five thousand square *amos*.[193] This excludes salty or brackish water. The *Dvar Shmuel*[194] does allow a *karpaf* consisting of planted fields within an *eruv* when the significance of the inhabited sector of the enclosure outweighs the significance of the uninhabited, planted sector. Most *Poskim* conclude, however, that the *Dvar Shmuel*'s leniency only applies to enclosures consisting of real walls. This ruling is, therefore, generally not relevant in modern urban settings. The *Divrei Malkiel*,[195] and others rule that if an *eruv* was built around an area that contained

---

192 Rabbi Akiva Yosef Kaplan noted that in the source of this Halacha, the *Chacham Tzvi, siman* 59, cited by the *Sha'arei Teshuva, Orach Chaim*, 358:8, it seems that it is not necessary that a pathway exist between the furrows, but rather only that it be possible to walk between the furrows. Rabbi Kaplan continued to posit that it seems sensible to assume that there must be a requirement of paths. Otherwise, there practically always exists at least some possibility of walking between the planted rows! Perhaps we might contemplate a "compromise" position: If a pathway exists, that certainly is sufficient. If no path exists, but permission can be secured from the owner of the property to walk at regular intervals through his field in ways that would diminish the "impassable" planted area to an area of less than *beis se'asayim*, that may nullify the *karpaf* problem as well. More extensive discussions concerning the necessity and width of the path are to be found in *Kesser Ephraim, siman* 43; *Hilchos Eruvin* 7:12 and note 165 there.

193 *Shulchan Aruch*, ibid., 358:11. See also *Mishna Berura* there, 358:85 and the *Sha'ar Ha'Tziyun* there, 358:80-81. It seems from the *Rashba*'s language that although in our times we rarely use pond or stream water for these purposes, nevertheless, where water is theoretically suitable for those purposes it is not considered a *karpaf*. This definition still excludes polluted or dirty bodies of water.

194 Cited in the *Biur Halacha* 358:9, *d.h. Aval Im Nizra*. The *Chacham Tzvi, siman* 59, also cited there by the *Biur Halacha*, extended the *Dvar Shmuel*'s leniency even to cases where a *tzuras ha'pesach* preceded the development of a *karpaf* (such as a planted field) within its perimeter. In the specific case discussed by the *Chacham Tzvi*, however, other mitigating factors were involved. See also *Nesivos Shabbos* 13:15 and note 50.

195 Vol. 4 *siman* 3.

a pre-existing *karpaf*, then the *"hekef l'dira"* (the act of enclosure for the purpose of enhancing human habitation) of the *eruv* enclosure counteracts the *eino mukaf l'dira* of the *karpaf*. Such an *eruv* is therefore valid. The case in question in that *teshuva*, however, concerned an area that was technically suitable for walking, however the gentile owner would not allow anyone to actually do so.

Furthermore, the *Divrei Malkiel* employs several additional reasons in validating the *eruv* that included this *karpaf*. It is therefore difficult to isolate one of his reasons and extrapolate a universal leniency based solely on that one reason.[196] The best solution is to exclude a questionable area from the *eruv*. Constructing a *tzuras ha'pesach* around the *karpaf* itself may accomplish this.

10. Delasos (Doors)

We have not dealt extensively with the construction of *eruvin* in true *reshuyos ha'rabbim*. As we have learnt (see Chapter II, Section 1), it is essentially impractical to construct such an *eruv*. Let us repeat: A street that is a *reshus ha'rabbim* must be rectified by means of doors of a type that Halacha regards as a true wall. Many modern *eruvin* employ some innovative form of *delasos*, such as tarpaulins wrapped around light poles that, at least theoretically, may be drawn across a street and close it off.[197] The parameters of *delasos*, however, are as laden with halachic contention as the parameters of *karpaf*. Questions center on the issues of the extent to which the doors must be actually closed (*"delasos hanin'alos ba'laila,"* literally: doors that are closed at night - a parameter whose minimal definition is the subject of some of the most intense controversy in *eruvin*), as opposed to suitable for closing. In practice, then, doors are usually used only as a *"snif"* (an

---

196 In *Hilchos Eruvin* 4:14, note 168, Rabbi Lange notes that the *Biur Halacha*, ibid., *d.h. HaZera'im Mevatlim HaDira* would apparently disagree with the *Divrei Malkiel*. Rabbi Lange therefore says that one may rely on the *Divrei Malkiel*'s heter only *"b'dochak gadol."* We have already noted that it is difficult to conceive of a *she'as ha'dechak* in a normal community setting, see above, note 138.

197 See, for example, *The Detroit Eruv*, pp. 17-18.

additional rationale for a lenient ruling) - to add weight to other factors that justify the construction of an *eruv* in the area in question.[198]

Frequently, however, even a "regular" *eruv* will make use of doors. This is prevalent where a fence comprises some part of the perimeter. Fences often have breaks to allow pedestrians and vehicles to enter and exit. As we have learnt, where these openings are wider than ten *amos*, they require some rectification. Often such openings have doors. If these doors are actually closed at night they fulfill without question the parameter of *delasos hanin'alos ba'laila*.[199]

The question, then, is whether one may rely on these *delasos* if they do not also possess a *tzuras ha'pesach* overhead as well. To a significant degree, this question revolves around the issue of the extent to which the rules and regulations of *eruvin* mimic those of *mezuza*. To qualify as a doorway that generates the requirement of a *mezuza*, an opening must possess both side posts and a lintel[200] (and, according to the Rambam,[201] a door as well). An opening (such as a gate to a backyard) that possesses sideposts and a door, but no lintel, does not require a *mezuza*. The *Chazon Ish* and others hold that the parameters are linked.[202] *Delasos* alone, without a *tzuras ha'pesach*,

198 See *Nesivos Shabbos*, all of chap. 23; *Noam*, vol. 21, pp. 42-92; and *Tzitz Eliezer* 14:90.

199 See *Yesodei Yeshurun*, ibid., pp. 318-324; and *Nesivos Shabbos* 23:1 and notes 9-10. The *Nesivos Shabbos* there notes that although in a true *reshus ha'rabbim* many *Poskim* hold that the doors must actually be closed at night; when the doors are part of an *eruv* enclosing a *carmelis*, they only need be *"re'uyos l'hina'el,"* suitable for closing. Thus, for example a gate in a fence that encloses a yard need not actually be closed to allow carrying within the yard - the fact that it is suitable for closing suffices.

200 *Shulchan Aruch, Yoreh De'ah,* 287:1.

201 *Mishne Torah, Hilchos Mezuza,* 6:1.

202 *Orach Chaim*, 78:1-5 and 79:9. The *Minchas Yitzchok* 6:34 posits that the *Chazon Ish* would only adhere to his stringent ruling where the *delasos* in question were: a) built to permit carrying in a true *reshus ha'rabbim*; and, b) never closed. According to the *Minchas Yitzchok*'s understanding, the *Chazon Ish*'s position

would not be valid enclosures.

The preponderance of *Poskim*, however, rule that *delasos* are valid enclosures even without *tzuros ha'pesach* overhead. That none of the primary sources of the parameters of *delasos* mention a requirement of an accompanying *tzuras ha'pesach* seems to serve as significant evidence for this position. This school of thought opines that *delasos* do not serve as enclosures because they fulfill parameters of doorways, but rather because of their capacity to block the traffic of passers-by.[203]

11. What if an Eruv Breaks or is Invalid?

It is customary to check a municipal *eruv* every *Erev Shabbos*.[204] What happens if subsequently, on *Shabbos*, it is discovered that the *eruv* is in fact invalid? Most *Poskim* rule that one should not attempt

---

would be more lenient in situations where the doors were originally constructed and are now used to block entrance to an area that would otherwise be a *carmelis* such as the gate of a yard (these parameters would then resemble those described by the *Nesivos Shabbos* vis-à-vis the issue of *re'uyos l'hina'el* that we discussed above in note 199). While the *Minchas Yitzchok* attempts to prove these distinctions from the text of the *Chazon Ish*, it is not clear that the *Chazon Ish* intended to infer such leniencies.

203 See, for example, *Eruvin* 6b and *Shulchan Aruch, Orach Chaim* 364:2. Some *Acharonim* base the fundamental distinction between the function of a *tzuras ha'pesach* (that a doorway is considered the equivalent of a wall) and *delasos* (that a capacity to block traffic is considered the equivalent of a wall) on the *Yerushalmi Eruvin* 1:1 (6a in the Vilna edition) where Rabbi Ba states that by means of a door *reshus ha'rabbim* is locked. Although he does not mention the *Yerushalmi*, the *Rashba* in *Avodas HaKodesh, Beis Nesivos* 2:4 (see also the *Avodas Avoda* - there note 47.) and 3:1, implies the distinct function of *delasos* very clearly. See also above, Chapter III, note 133. The *Nesivos Shabbos*, ibid., note 16, cites the *Chasam Sofer, Avnei Nezer* and others, including the aforementioned *Minchas Yitzchok*, who rule leniently on this issue. See also *Yesodei Yeshurun*, ibid., who also cites the famous work of the Radziner Rebbe, Rabbi Gershon Chanoch Leiner (the *"Ba'al HaTecheles"*) allowing construction of *eruvin* based on *delasos* in the significant number of European cities that did not allow construction of *tzuros ha'pesach*.

204 See note 181 above.

to notify the population of this development. The reason they cite for this ruling is the principle of *"mutav sheyeeheyu shoggegin v'al yeeheyu mezidin"* - since many people will be skeptical of a declaration that the *eruv* has become invalid and will carry anyway, better that they remain unaware of their sin than that they be made aware of the possible problem and sin intentionally.[205] I have heard from my great-uncle, Rabbi Yosef Dov Holzberg, that Rabbi Chaim Soloveichik in Brisk ruled similarly, but for a different reason. Reb Chaim's rationale was that people who carry under the mistaken impression that the *eruv* is valid fall into the halachic category of *"mis'asek."* A *mis'asek* is one who commits any forbidden act thinking that it is permissible. When it comes to *Hilchos Shabbos*, where only *"meleches machasheves"* - intentional activity - is prohibited, a *mis'asek*'s "misdeeds" are not considered sinful at all, and do not require *Teshuva*.[206] Since the people that are carrying do so because they think that the *eruv* is still valid, they are committing no wrong.

This leads us to an interesting question. Even if a city's *eruv* is not valid, why bother fixing it or informing others that it is invalid? If the *Rav Ha'Machshir* and whoever else knows that the *eruv* is invalid do not carry, everyone else should be considered *mis'asek*, and thus are not liable for carrying! The *Poskim* discuss the related issue of a new communal Rabbi taking over the supervision of an *eruv*, built by his predecessor, that is clearly invalid. Must the new Rabbi immediately pronounce the *eruv* invalid?[207] Clearly, very basic issues of public *emes* (Torah-true truth) and *sheker* (falsehood) are involved in such circumstances. In each subjective situation a *Posek* must be consulted.

---

205 See *Nesivos Shabbos* 15:37 and note 37.

206 See *Shemiras Shabbos K'Hilchasa* 17:25 and note 109; vol. 3 p. 29 and 1:29 and note 118. Rabbi Yehoshua Neuwirth advises telling those one is sure will listen that the *eruv* is down. Rabbi Shlomo Zalman Auerbach, however, seems inclined toward the tradition cited in the name of Reb Chaim. See also Rabbi Elchonon Wasserman's *Kovetz Shiurim* vol. 2, *siman* 23.

207 Rabbi Hershel Schachter in *HaPardes*, year 63, 1:3. He does not discuss the principle of *mis'asek*, but the similar concept that unintentional transgressions of rabbinic prohibitions (*shogeg bidi'rabbanan*) do not require *Teshuva*. A discussion of this topic may be found in Rabbi Yosef Engel's *Asvan D'oraysa, siman* 10.

Note that the *Maharshal* states that willful falsification and distortion of Torah precepts is a capital offense.[208]

12. Chapter Conclusion

It is to be hoped that we understand by now the extraordinary complexities that are the very nature of these Halachos. It is, furthermore, imperative to consider the specific nature of the terrain, equipment, and appearances of each and every subjective situation that may generate questions. It is therefore crucial and essential to insure that a competent rabbinic authority well versed in *Hilchos Eruvin* personally inspects a communal *eruv* at regular intervals.[209] Details related verbally to a *Posek* may not accurately portray the circumstances of the case, leading to inaccurate rulings.[210]

---

208 *Yam shel Shlomo, Bava Kamma* 38a.

209 Unfortunately, even smaller *eruvin* are not problem free. See, for example, articles by Rabbi Yosef Wikler in the Summer 1988 and June 1991 issues of *Kashrus Magazine* that discuss the many problems that frequently arise in bungalow colony *eruvin*. We must clearly note and understand that we have not come even close to an exhaustive review of all the Halachos and potential problems of *tzuras ha'pesach* and related components of an *eruv*. A more comprehensive picture can be obtained by perusing the entire 19th chapter of *Nesivos Shabbos* and the entire fourth chapter of *Hilchos Eruvin*.

210 A good "How To" guide describing in detail (down to where to buy materials!) many practical solutions to various problems that arise in the construction of urban *eruvin* is Dr. Bert Miller's *The Baltimore Eruv* (Baltimore, 1981).

Chapter V

RENTING THE AREA FROM THE AUTHORITIES AND ERUVEI CHATZEIROS IN MULTIPLE UNIT DWELLINGS AND HOTELS

1. Eruvei Chatzeiros vs. Sechiras Reshus: What, Which, When?

Me'd'oraysa the ownership of an area is not relevant to the prohibition of carrying on *Shabbos* and *Yom Tov*. The halachic status of an area as a *reshus ha'yachid, reshus ha'rabbim*, or *carmelis* is determined *me'd'oraysa* solely on the basis of the nature of the enclosure - or lack thereof - surrounding it. *Chazal*, however, specified that not only must a *reshus ha'yachid* be enclosed but, in addition, all the residents in the enclosed area must form a symbolic unified entity.[211] Only then is carrying therein allowed. Since this requirement is only *me'd'rabbanan, Chazal* were lenient and only required symbolic, not actual, unified ownership of the area in question. Depending on whom the other partner/s in the area in question is/are, one or two methods must be employed in achieving the symbolic unified ownership: *"eruvei chatzeiros"* or *"sechiras reshus."*

Eruvei chatzeiros (literally: the merging of the courtyards) works in one of the two following manners: Pieces of bread (or, better yet, if one does not want to repeat the procedure often, *matzo* - it remains edible longer) are collected from every family within the *eruv* and placed in one of the houses within the *eruv*.[212] This act, together with the appropriate verbal formula, enables us to symbolically view all the residents of the area as if they have united and all now dwell in the house in which the *eruv chatzeiros*, i.e., the collection of bread, is

---

211 See above, Chapter I, Section 1. Vacant dwellings need not be included in the *eruvei chatzeiros* or *sechiras reshus*. Only current residents must participate.

212 *Shulchan Aruch, Orach Chaim* 366:1.

kept. If it is not feasible or convenient to collect pieces of bread from all the families in the area, one person may take his own loaf of bread and grant the other residents ownership of it by way of the halachic device of *"zechiah"* (literally: bestowing ownership).[213] This procedure is relatively simple, and readily accessible in such common sources as the *Kitzur Shulchan Aruch*.[214] (We should note that the *zechiah* procedure requires two people: The *"mezakkeh"* - the owner of the loaf who confers upon the others ownership therein; and the *"zocheh"* - a person who acts as the agent of those others who are acquiring ownership through the *zechiah*.[215])

If up to eighteen families reside within the area in question, each must possess a minimum amount (*"shiur"*) of at least the size of a *grogeres* (a dried fig, which is approximately one third to one half the size of an egg)[216] in the bread of the *eruvei chatzeiros*. Eighteen *grogeros* is the maximum required *shiur*. No matter how many more families reside in the area, no more than eighteen *grogeros* are required to unify them with the *eruvei chatzeiros* (ibid.).

There are various opinions as to the length of time for which an *eruvei chatzeiros* remains in effect. Prevalent custom is (as long as the bread used has not been eaten and remains edible) to renew the *eruvei chatzeiros* annually.[217] Nevertheless, if *kosher l'Pesach* matzos

---

213 Ibid., 366:9.

214 94:6-7.

215 Those now acquiring ownership need not actively appoint the *zocheh* as their agent. The operative principle is *"zachin l'adam shelo b'fanav"* (literally: one may bestow ownership on another without that person's awareness). Where acquiring an object is advantageous for a person, his explicit consent to the acquisition is not necessary (*Kiddushin* 42a). See *Shulchan Aruch*, ibid., 366:10 for the preferences as to who should be involved in the *zechiah* process, and that, if it is impossible to find anyone else, one may perform the procedure with one's wife or adult children, even if they are members of the same household.

216 *Shulchan Aruch*, ibid.,368:3.

217 While the *eruvei chatzeiros* may remain valid for an extended period, it suffices as long as it was properly in effect Friday evening at twilight. In fact, it was the custom of the *Arizal* to make the *hamotzi* Friday night on the loaf used for *shitufei*

are used, then the *eruvei chatzeiros* can be valid for even longer - until the matzos are no longer edible.[218]

Sechiras reshus (literally: rental of domain) is a completely different procedure. It, too, however, is relatively simple and clearly explained by the *Kitzur Shulchan Aruch*.[219] In *sechiras reshus*, the person who would like to carry in an enclosed area on *Shabbos* asks the residents or owners of the other dwellings in the area to rent to him the right to carry in the area in question. Since here, too, the acquisition of the right is symbolic in nature, the rent paid may be symbolic as well. (I was once present at a ceremony in which the right to carry in a town was rented from the town council for twenty years for one dollar.)[220]

We require *eruvei chatzeiros* in most cases in which an *eruv* includes two or more *Shomer Shabbos* (*Shabbos* observant) Jewish residents. *Sechiras Reshus* is necessary when the *eruv* includes residents who are not *Shomrei Shabbos* - either because they are not Jewish or because they are not observant.[221]

---

mevo'os and then to make *hamotzi Shabbos* morning on the loaf designated for *eruvei chatzeiros* - *Yesodei Yeshurun, Ma'areches Lamed Tes Melachos*, vol. 2, p. 330.

218 *Shulchan Aruch*, ibid., 368:5.

219 94:18-23.

220 Rabbi Akiva Yosef Kaplan pointed out that while I wrote that the "rental" aspect of *sechiras reshus* pertains to the right to carry in the area being rented, specifying this definition is not essential. The language of the *Shulchan Aruch*, ibid., 382:4 is (free translation):

> If one who rents from a non-Jew without specification [of the extent of the rights being rented] this is effective, as one does not have to specify that the rental is to permit carrying. One also need not put the rental in writing.

See *Nesivos Shabbos* 37:28 and notes 95-99 for further information on the length of time for which a *sechiras reshus* is valid. See also *Yesodei Yeshurun*, ibid., pp. 314-315.

221 See *Shulchan Aruch*, ibid., 385:1 and the *Mishna Berura* there, 385:1. See also

2. *Some Practical Applications*

Let us explore these parameters by way of two sample cases: A duplex, i.e., a building in which two families live; and a triplex, i.e., a building in which three families live.

If both resident families of a duplex are *Shomrei Shabbos, eruvei chatzeiros* is required to carry from common areas to private areas (and vice versa) and from one resident's private area to another resident's private area.[222] If, however, only one of the families is *Shomer Shabbos,* then that family utilizes neither *eruvei chatzeiros* nor *sechiras reshus*. Carrying on *Shabbos* within the enclosed area shared by the two families is allowed here without any additional procedure pertaining to the halachic "ownership" of the area. The *Gemara* explains that, strictly speaking, the domain of a non-*Shomer Shabbos* resident should not prevent a fellow resident from carrying on *Shabbos* within the enclosed area that they share.[223] The purpose of *eruvei chatzeiros* was to unify all the *Shomrei Shabbos* in the vicinity. Thus, only the presence of fellow residents who are *Shomrei Shabbos* generates the requirement of *eruvei chatzeiros.* Nevertheless, to discourage *Shomrei Shabbos* from living near non-Jews, *Chazal*

---

the *Chazon Ish, Orach Chaim* 87:14; *Hilchos Eruvin* 8:17-20; and, *Nesivos Shabbos* 36:24-28 for additional discussions and parameters of situations where Jews who are not *Shomer Shabbos* are involved. The *Chazon Ish* differentiates between informed Jews who are familiar with the Halachos of *Shabbos*, yet do not observe them, with whom *sechiras reshus* must be contracted, and "*tinokos shenishbu*" - Jews who do not observe *Shabbos* because they grew up in ignorance of its parameters, who should be included in an *eruv chatzeiros.* Prevailing practice, in such cases, is to implement both procedures. See below, note 224.

222 See *Shemiras Shabbos K'Hilchasa* 17:11-12.

223 *Eruvin* 62a; *Shulchan Aruch, Orach Chaim,* 382:1 and *Biur Halacha*, ibid., *d.h. Az Hanochri.* A potential consequence of this Halacha applies if one has the misfortune to land in an airport (outside the State of Israel) after *Shabbos* has begun. If, as often happens, one can walk within an uninterrupted enclosed area from the airplane, through the terminal, to an attached hotel, one may carry one's luggage the entire way. Different authorities might own these areas. Since, however, their status is one of exclusive non-Jewish ownership, no *sechiras reshus* is necessary to carry from one area to another.

subsequently instituted a new requirement: that the *Shomer Shabbos* resident must rent the right to carry from his non-Jewish fellow resident (*sechiras reshus*). *Chazal* hoped that the non-Jew would regard such a request by his neighbor as suspicious and dangerous, and deny the request. The observant neighbor would then be in the uncomfortable situation of not being able to carry on *Shabbos*. We would thus induce him to move away from the courtyard that he had shared with the non-Jew. This requirement was applied to an enclosed area shared with a non-*Shomer Shabbos* Jew as well.

As with many *"gezeiros d'rabbanan"* (rabbinic decrees), *"milsa d'lo shechicha lo gazru ba rabbanan"* - our Rabbis did not extend their decrees to rare cases. At the time of *Chazal*, solitary Jews or Jewish families rarely resided with non-Jewish neighbors. *Ovdei kochavim* (pagan idolators) of the time were suspect of murder. Were two Jewish families not in close enough proximity to check upon each other regularly, there would be a real fear that non-Jewish neighbors would take advantage of the isolation of a single Jewish family and murder them. *Chazal*, therefore, did not extend the requirement of *sechiras reshus* to such uncommon cases. The Halacha remains that whenever a single Jewish individual or family shares the enclosed area with any number of non-Jews, no *sechiras reshus* is required.[224]

In the case of a triplex, there are several possible configurations: a) Three Jewish families; b) Two Jewish (*Shomer Shabbos*) families and one non-Jewish family; c) One Jewish family and two non-Jewish families. In the first configuration only *eruvei chatzeiros* among the three families is required. In the second configuration we would require the two Jewish families to make an *eruvei chatzeiros* between themselves and to contract a *sechiras reshus* from the non-Jewish family as well. In the third configuration we would require no additional procedures at all. The solitary Jewish family needs make neither *eruvei chatzeiros* nor *sechiras reshus*. We can easily apply the

224 Although the Halacha of a *Mechalel Shabbos* is like that of a non-Jew in many aspects of *Hilchos Eruvin*, *sechiras reshus* may be required where a solitary *Shomer Shabbos* lives with one or more *Mechalelei Shabbos*. See the *Nesivos Shabbos* cited in note 221. As noted, in practice, when confronted with such a situation, the observant individual should both contract *sechiras reshus* and perform *eruvei chatzeiros* (without a *bracha*).

principles that we have just outlined to apartment buildings and other situations where more people reside together within an enclosed area.

When one must deal with many *Shomer Shabbos* residents, the procedure remains relatively simple. One individual can make an *eruvei chatzeiros* of eighteen *grogeros* for unlimited amounts of people by way of *zechiah*. When, however, one must deal with large amounts of non-Jews or non-observant Jews, a major difficulty arises: It is not necessarily advantageous for someone to have a right rented from him, and therefore *zechiah* cannot work here. To contract a *sechiras reshus* from every non-Jewish or non-observant resident of a large apartment building, or every guest in a hotel, would be prohibitively difficult. It would be even more difficult to contract a *sechiras reshus* from all the inhabitants of an area surrounded by a large urban eruv! There are two distinct solutions to this problem, depending on the situation in question.

3. *Sechiras Reshus from a Landlord*

The *Rashba* writes:[225]

> [When] large ships [are] divided into rooms that are rented to various travelers, each in his own room, if among them are two Jews in separate rooms who eat separately [who wish to carry on *Shabbos*], they cannot do so... for *eruv* and *bittul*[226] are not effective in the presence of non-Jews.
>
> What is their solution? They should rent the right to carry throughout the ship from its owner before he distributes the

---

225 *Avodas HaKodesh, Beis Nesivos*, 4:8 (in Rabbi C. G. Tzimbalist's edition, vol. 2, p. 152).

226 Literally: nullification, a third manner of unifying separate *reshuyos ha'yachid*. Where *eruvei chatzeiros* was not performed before *Shabbos* began, one or more of the other Jewish residents of the enclosed area may nullify their domains in favor of one of the residents on *Shabbos*. The latter resident and members of his or her household may then carry throughout the area, but the others may not. This is obviously not a very advantageous means of unification, and is therefore rarely used. The Halachos of *bittul* are to be found in *Shulchan Aruch*, ibid., 380-381.

rooms among the other passengers. If they did not do *sechiras reshus* before the rooms were distributed to the other passengers, they cannot subsequently rent the right to carry from the ship's owner. This is because the primary authority becomes the renter [the passenger], as we have explained.[227] If, however, the ship's owner retains the right to place objects throughout the ship, even in the rooms rented to passengers, then the Jewish passengers only have to contract *sechiras reshus* from the ship's owner, just as one may contract *sechiras reshus* from the employee or agent of the owner of an area.[228]

The *Rashba* refers us to a previous ruling:

When a non-Jew rents his property to another non-Jew, if the owner retains the right to remove the tenant whenever he wants, then *sechiras reshus* may be done from the owner - even if he has not removed the tenant yet. [There are two reasons why this is the Halacha,] because the *sechiras reshus* is itself a form of removal, and because [under such circumstances] the owner is the primary authority. If, however, the owner cannot remove the tenant, then the *sechiras reshus* must contracted with the tenant. It seems to me that if, however, the owner has some control over the property he has rented to the tenant, such as objects stored on that property, or even just the right to place objects on the property, then one may even rent the right to carry from the owner, who is then no worse than the employee or agent of the tenant.

These rulings of the *Rashba* are codified as accepted practice in the *Shulchan Aruch*.[229] Control of an owner over property through the placement of objects is known as *"tefisas yad"* (literally: under the

227 *Avodas HaKodesh*, 4:3 (ibid., p. 69).

228 See *Avodas Avoda, Tosefes Biur*, 4:28.

229 *Shulchan Aruch*, ibid., 382:18,19. See the *Mishna Berura* there, *se'ifim ketanim* 60-64 and *se'ifim ketanim* 75-77.

control of one's hand).

Based on the principles that we find in these passages in the *Avodas HaKodesh*, Rabbi Moshe Feinstein rules that whenever a landlord owns objects in the tenants' apartments that the tenants may not remove without permission (refrigerators, stoves, etc.), one may contract the requisite *sechiras reshus* with the landlord, and does not have to approach each individual tenant.[230] This, in Reb Moshe's opinion, is true even if the tenant has rented the right to use the objects in question. The basis of this ruling, as the *Rashba* explained, is that through the ownership of the objects in each tenant's apartment, the owner retains some authority over the rented apartments. This enables the landlord to contract an umbrella *sechiras reshus* for all the properties that the landlord owns.[231]

This ruling has more, very important, practical consequences. For example, let us take a case of a *Shomer Shabbos* landlord who lives in the same building as his tenants. If this landlord owns and provides refrigerators to all the tenants, then according to Reb Moshe's logic, neither *eruvei chatzeiros* nor *sechiras reshus* would be necessary. All the tenants are unified with the landlord by way of the *tefisas yad*. Similarly, in the case of a hotel, as long as the owner of the hotel, his agent, or his employee resides in the hotel, all the guests are considered unified through *tefisas yad*. Neither *eruvei chatzeiros* nor

---

230 *Igros Moshe, Orach Chaim* 1:141.

231 We should note that other *Poskim*, most notably the Kovner Rav, *Dvar Avraham* 3:30 (who is not sure whether objects rented to the tenant still manifest the owner's control), the *Chazon Ish*, ibid., *siman* 92 (who assumes without question that rented objects do <u>not</u> manifest the owner's control), and the *Chelkas Ya'akov* 1:207 are not in agreement with Reb Moshe on this point. In fact, in reaching his conclusion, Reb Moshe differs with a *Mishna Berura*. Nevertheless, Reb Moshe's logic and evidence in this regard are very strong. Reb Moshe writes that objects of the types provided by the landlord to the tenant in our times are not completely at the disposal of the tenant. The tenant, for example, is not free to remove those objects from the premises without permission. Such restrictions that manifest the landlord's control constitute proper *tefisas yad*. It is possible that the *Chazon Ish* would accept this approach as well. The case discussed by the *Chazon Ish* is one in which the tenants may have had the right to reject and remove the objects in question.

sechiras reshus would be necessary.[232]

It is important to stress that many *Poskim* hold that for *tefisas yad* to suffice, the landlord him - or her - self or an employee of the landlord must reside in the building. If the landlord lives off the premises, then *eruvei chatzeiros* and/or *sechiras reshus* is still necessary. One may, however, still make a single umbrella *sechiras reshus* through the landlord. In these cases additional measures are necessary because the units (apartments or hotel rooms) to be unified must all be considered consolidated in one of the residences on the premises. This symbolism requires that the person who facilitates this unification reside within the area or on the premises that are being unified.[233]

4. Sechiras Reshus in Public and Urban Areas

The various procedures that we have examined are applicable when dealing with privately owned properties: buildings, yards, and the like.[234] Let us say, however, for example, that one wants to make

---

232 Even those *Poskim* who disagree with Reb Moshe and do not consider objects that the tenant or guest uses sufficient *tefisas yad* entertain the possibility that where the hotel management retains the right to switch the guests' room, that itself is sufficient control. *Sechiras reshus* and *eruvei chatzeiros* would not be required. See *Nesivos Shabbos* 34:7 and note 25. See also the *Mishna Berura* 370:33 and the *Biur Halacha* there *d.h. Einam Osrim*. If the owner can evict the tenant any time he pleases, everyone agrees that no further procedures are required.

233 Additional Halachos of *tefisas yad* are found in the *Shulchan Aruch*, ibid., 370:2 and *Nesivos Shabbos* 27:12-16. We should note that the landlord's objects in the tenant's residence must be of a type that cannot be removed on *Shabbos*, either because they are *muktzeh* or because they are so heavy that they are not normally moved. Furthermore, the <u>right</u> to place objects in the tenant's residence is insufficient. Actual objects must be in place in order to utilize the mechanism of *tefisas yad*. I have heard from several reliable sources that Reb Moshe did <u>not</u> require that the landlord or his employee reside in the building or complex in order that *tefisas yad* should suffice. He held that, halachically, the landlord is considered to reside in <u>all</u> the complex's apartments. There is a prevalent practice to rely on this tradition. I have been unable, however, to find this ruling in any of Reb Moshe's printed *teshuvos*.

234 An important note: Neighbors who would like to make an *eruv* between their properties must have a halachically valid opening between their properties. For

an *eruv* with one's neighbor who lives across the street. They may unify their respective properties through *eruvei chatzeiros*; they may include any non-Jew's property in their *eruv* by way of *sechiras reshus*; but what about the street itself? A public thoroughfare does not belong to any particular person - with whom does one contract the *sechiras reshus*?[235]

---

example, if two neighbors want to make an *eruv* that encompasses two yards separated by a fence, there must be an opening in that fence in order for them to make an *eruv* together. That opening must be within the area encompassed by their eruv. The fact that they can pass things over the fence (or through a window) to each other is not enough of a connection. There is an exception to this rule. "*Keilim sheshavsu bechatzeir*" - objects that were in a yard from before *Shabbos* - may be passed to another yard (or to a roof, but not to the street or any other *carmelis*) without *eruvei chatzeiros*. See *Shulchan Aruch*, ibid., 372:1,4. If there is a proper opening, and an *eruv* is made, the neighbors may then also pass objects that were inside their respective houses to each other over the fence as well (*Mishna Berura* 372:29).

235 Although streets are not residences, if passers-by possess the right to pass unimpeded through the *eruv* on those streets, then they must be rented from the proper authorities. See *Chavos Yair, siman* 135, cited briefly in the *Be'eir Heitev* and *Sha'arei Teshuva, Orach Chaim*, 391:1. See also the *Mishna Berura* 391:13-14 and the *Nesivos Shabbos* 37:27-28.

(We should note that it is possible to mistakenly infer from the *Be'eir Heitev* that one may carry in a non-Jewish walled city without *sechiras reshus*. The *Chavos Yair* rules explicitly to the contrary. I should also note that I was once challenged by an individual who maintained that the *Chavos Yair* only required *sechiras reshus* in the case of an *eruv* constructed on a specific street inhabited exclusively by Jews within a larger walled city inhabited by non-Jews as well. This individual posited that only the presence of non-Jewish homes within an *eruv* mandated *sechiras reshus*. The nature of a walled city is such that any area within it is considered a *reshus ha'yachid*, which, this individual opined, is tantamount to a home. He claimed that this is not applicable to modern metropolitan areas. This argument is clearly in error on several counts. Let us examine two. First, *the Chavos Yair clearly* discusses the case of an *eruv* constructed on a specific street inhabited by Jews within a larger walled city because that was the case in question. He does not indicate that it is the wall that is the catalyst for the requirement of *sechiras reshus*, rather, he states that because a wall surrounds the larger area, he cannot understand why the smaller *eruv* is necessary. The reason that the streets generate a requirement of *sechiras reshus* is that they allow free passage ("*derisas regel ha'oseres*") to individuals not included in the communal *eruvei chatzeiros* or *shitufei mevo'os*, as discussed in the *Shulchan Aruch*, ibid., 378:2 and 382:3. Secondly, if a wall generates a *reshus ha'yachid* for the purposes of this Halacha, then a *tzuras ha'pesach* generates the same parameters.

In the same vein, as we have mentioned, when an *eruv* encompasses a large area that includes many houses and buildings, it is next to impossible to contract a *sechiras reshus* from each and every homeowner or landlord in the area. How can we undertake *sechiras reshus* in such situations?

Although we have posed these two problems together, the solution to the first problem is far less complex. Where *sechiras reshus* must be done on a public area such as a street, one goes to a person that can control access to the street and contracts the *sechiras reshus* from that person, his agent, or his employee. A prevalent practice is to contract the *sechiras reshus* from the police who have the authority to manipulate traffic on the streets. It is preferable to go to a commissioner or another high ranking official who has actual jurisdiction over the streets in question. One may, however, also approach a regular officer - who falls into the category of an agent or employee of the higher official.[236] I have heard in the past of *eruv* committees contracting *sechiras reshus* from officials such as the Borough Presidents of New York City.[237] Some rabbinic authorities

---

Sidewalks, however, may not fall into the same category as streets. Some rabbinic authorities hold that where the residents either legally own the sidewalks; the residents have rights to limit use of the sidewalks; or, the residents bear responsibility for the maintenance of the sidewalk, that these are sufficient forms of control. *Sechiras reshus* from the authorities would not be required in such cases.

236 *Shulchan Aruch*, ibid., 391:1; *Chazon Ish*, ibid., 82:9. The *Chazon Ish* writes that the logic behind this Halacha is not that the municipal authorities are akin to landlords. Rather, their authority to control the areas in question is similar to *tefisas yad*. They are therefore, in effect, the agents and employees of whoever the true halachic owner might be - here, the citizenry of the city. (See below in this Section, a similar rationale advanced by the *Tikvas Zecharia*.)

237 See *Nesivos Shabbos* 37:27, note 93. In Israel it is preferable to contract the *sechiras reshus* with a police officer, who represents a national level of authority, than from the mayor, who represents only a municipal level of authority. The *Nesivos Shabbos* also notes that certain areas, such as embassies of foreign nations, are not subject to any form of the host country's jurisdiction. Therefore, no umbrella *sechiras reshus* will be effective for these areas. See also *Mishna Berura* 391:18 and *Hilchos Eruvin* 8:21 note 208, that renting from the police is preferable to renting from the army.

have questioned this practice, since these officials may not be empowered to authorize street closings.

This *sechiras reshus* is effective for the problem of public areas (streets, parks, etc.). But what about the second problem, the myriad distinct private *reshuyos* for which an umbrella *sechiras reshus* must be made? Ironically, in totalitarian countries, where authorities can enter houses and place objects or soldiers therein at will, the solution is simple: We deem the right of entry and placement as a form of *tefisas yad*, enabling the Jewish community to contract an effective umbrella *sechiras reshus* with the authorities for the entire area within an *eruv*. In most democratic countries, however, the government may not enter a private home at will. They surely cannot store objects or quarter soldiers on the premises except under extraordinary circumstances. What, then, enables us to contract an umbrella *sechiras reshus* in such situations?

The *Chazon Ish*[238] seems to hold that the police's right of entry is a sufficient measure of control to contract from them an umbrella *sechiras reshus*:

> ...Because they are considered like employees that possess authority in the entire area for the government's needs.

This right is tantamount to the police having borrowed space in each resident's dwelling.[239]

---

[238] Ibid., 82:9. The quotation that follows is from that *siman*. I am indebted to Rabbi Shraga Rothbart for noting that my original phrasing here was inaccurate. See also *Yesodei Yeshurun*, ibid., pp. 310-313.

[239] The *Chazon Ish* there, however, has other difficulties with the procedure of urban umbrella *sechiras reshus*. See also 82:34, and *Nesivos Shabbos*, ibid., note 94.

In the previous editions we wrote here: "Whether one relies on this ruling of the *Chazon Ish* or not, we should note that the issue of private residences does not affect the *heter* to carry in the streets of the city, concerning which the control of the authorities is complete. One would then be allowed to carry from and into the houses of all the *Shomrei Shabbos* included in the *eruv* (permitted by way of the *eruvei chatzeiros*), and throughout all the public areas within the city. If one wants to carry into buildings or yards within which non-Jews live, he may personally contract *sechiras reshus* with the people involved."

Years earlier, the *Tikvas Zecharia* succinctly summarized the basis of modern *sechiras reshus*. In the last paragraph of the following citation, he also provides a novel rationale for umbrella *sechiras reshus*:[240]

> The *Rivash* in *siman* 427 writes that it is possible to contract a *sechiras reshus* from the city's mayor, because he can place objects in the homes of the city's residents as he pleases. The *Rivash* also cites another rationale to allow the acquisition of jurisdiction from that mayor: Since the major thoroughfares are always under the mayor's authority and he may alter them as he pleases and require the residents to travel in a different manner, he obviously has the right to bar all the non-Jews from the thoroughfares. Since he may remove them, he also may sell their jurisdictions [over the streets]. The *Rivash* notes that the second reason will not suffice to permit carrying from the houses that belong to the non-Jews into the streets and vice versa. He therefore concludes that it is best to limit one's carrying to taking objects from houses owned by Jews into the streets and vice versa, and to refrain from carrying in and out of the houses of non-Jews. Based on these words of the *Rivash*, it is possible to analyze the rulings of the *Shulchan Aruch* and

---

This passage was based on the *Nesivos Shabbos* 37:27 and notes 93-94, who in turn based his ruling on the *Rama* in the *Shulchan Aruch*, ibid., 391:1.

This opinion assumes that unlike *karpeifos* (see above, Chapter III, Section 9), the private yards and open spaces belonging to non-Jews and *Mechalelei Shabbos* would not prohibit others from carrying in the streets and other areas, even if they are not surrounded by fences. See *Shulchan Aruch*, ibid., 382:3, the *Mishna Berura* there, *se'if katan* 19; and *Nesivos Shabbos* 36:7. A non-Jew's ownership would only prevent Jews from carrying in the specific area under his control - for which *sechiras reshus* would then be necessary. Adjacent areas in which carrying is allowed through *eruvei chatzeiros* or *sechiras reshus* would not be affected.

Rabbi Akiva Yosef Kaplan, however, noted that it is entirely possible that the *Rama*'s ruling pertains specifically to scenarios where the non-Jewish owned domains are in fact walled or otherwise halachically distinct from the area of the *eruv*. The *Chazon Ish* himself does not explicitly extend this concept to open, non-distinct areas owned by non-Jews included in an *eruv*.

240 *Tikvas Zecharia* pp. 39-40.

Rama in *siman* 391, and what the *Taz* writes there.

The *Pri Megadim, Mishbetzos Zahav* there, *se'if katan* 6, based on the *Tosafos Shabbos* and *Eliyahu Rabba*, writes that as far as we are concerned each reason is sufficient by itself. Therefore, when [the mayor] is authorized to quarter soldiers in private homes one is allowed to carry even to and from non-Jewish homes. If, however, [the mayor] is not authorized to do so, one may only carry to and from the Jewish homes into the streets.

Thus, according to the laws of this country that authorize the authorities to condemn private homes to construct roads, marketplaces, or other public uses when they deem necessary, the *Rivash*'s second reason will allow carrying even to and from non-Jewish homes into the streets.

According to the laws of this country magistrates can issue warrants allowing the police to enter any house (and, if the residents prevent them from doing so, they may break down the doors). Detectives can enter houses even without the knowledge of the homeowners. The officials in charge of hygiene and health may enter any house anytime to inspect the cleanliness, the water pipes and other matters, and then require the homeowners to work and fix any problems according to their directives. If the owner does not fulfill their directives, they can send workers with tools into the homes to make the repairs at the owners expense. If he does not reimburse the authorities, thay have the right to sell his house. All this suggests, in my humble opinion, that one may contract the *sechiras reshus* with the mayor of the city.

Furthermore, since the officials, the police officers, and all the city authorities involved in municipal matters, [such as] preventing harm, maintaining roads and preserving sanitation, are not appointed by a government, but rather elected by the inhabitants of the city that in turn are the sole source of their salaries, the municipal authorities and workers are thus no less than agents and employees of the inhabitants of the city, or, at the very least, they are agents and employees of agents and employees [and, therefore, *sechiras reshus* from the municipal authorities is tantamount to contracting *sechiras reshus* from each and every resident of the city].

It is questionable whether the last reason could stand on its own, as an elected official is not precisely identical to the employee of a corporation or private concern, but it may be sufficient to constitute an additional rationale for the lenient approach.

We must note that there are very significant questions surrounding the efficacy of the customary umbrella *sechiras reshus*. An example of a problem involved in the procedure is the following question, raised by the *Chazon Ish*:[241] If, at the time that an *eruv* is constructed, a *Shomer Shabbos* Jew owns a dwelling, it falls under the *eruvei chatzeiros* component of the procedures employed to permit carrying within the city. Let us say that subsequently the Jew sells the dwelling and a non-Jew then acquires it. It must then be "switched" to the *sechiras reshus* category. How does that switch occur automatically? Such switches - back and forth - will be necessary innumerable times during the course of an *eruv*'s effective lifespan.

Nevertheless, hundreds, perhaps thousands, of *eruvin* have been construced in urban areas since the time of King Solomon. Unlike the *reshus ha'rabbim* issues that, as we previously noted (Chapter II, Section 3), are of relatively recent vintage, the issues of *eruvei chatzeiros* and *sechiras reshus* have always been relevant and prevalent. Time-honored tradition is then, evidently, to incline toward leniency in these areas of concern.

5. *Chapter Conclusion*

We must emphasize that this Chapter is not meant to serve as a comprehensive analysis of the intricacies of *sechiras reshus* for urban areas! We mean it only as an overview of the issues and procedures involved. Authorities in the laws of *eruvin* must carefully consider whom to contact and how to contract with them the *sechiras reshus*

241 *Chazon Ish*, ibid., 82:34; *Nesivos Shabbos*, ibid., note 94. See, in this regard, the *Yesodei Yeshurun*, cited above, note 220.

for an urban area - and then, of course, go on to enact the *eruv chatzeiros* as well.

AFTERWORD

As we have seen (Chapter I, Section 1), the *Gemara*[242] relates that King Solomon enacted the decree requiring *eruvin* to allow carrying on *Shabbos*. Rabbi Tzadok *HaKohen* of Lublin[243] draws a parallel between this accomplishment and King Solomon's major accomplishment - building the *Beis HaMikdosh*, the Holy Temple. The *Beis HaMikdosh* was intended to create a set, defined and permanent space in which we would perceive *Hashem's* spiritual light. In a larger sense, all *eruvin* are intended for that purpose - to encompass *reshus ha'rabbim* in *reshus ha'yachid*. In a sense, therefore, an *eruv* elevates the area it encloses. Viewed from that perspective, the construction of an *eruv* implies a great responsibility, similar to the awesome responsibility involved in constructing the *Beis HaMikdosh*.

The *Maharal* of Prague[244] says that the focal *Meleches Shabbos* is *Hotza'a*, the prohibition on carrying. It follows that we must exercise the utmost caution in any attempt to allow carrying on *Shabbos*.

We therefore repeat: Our purpose in this work was not to provide practical halachic conclusions. Our intent is to familiarize contemporary *Shomrei Shabbos* with some of the many intricate details involved in *Hilchos Eruvin*.

We have seen (Chapter II, Section 1) that many sources stress the advisability and importance of building *eruvin* wherever possible.[245] Many *Poskim* exhibit a very positive attitude toward *eruvin*. The positive attitude in theory does not, however, always translate into a

---

242 *Eruvin* 21b.

243 *Dover Tzedek, siman* 4 (3a).

244 *Chiddushei Gur Aryeh*, beginning of *Messeches Shabbos*.

245 Besides the sources already quoted above, see also, *Shemiras Shabbos K'Hilchasa* 17:21; *Halachos of the Eruv*, "BeMakom Hakdama;" and *Yesodei Yeshurun, Ma'areches Lamed Tes Melachos*, vol. 2, p. 237 and p. 312.

positive attitude in practice. Our discussions should have clarified the reasons for this inconsistency. The possible pitfalls involved in the construction of even small *eruvin* are great and many. The nature of the Halachos of *eruvin* is such that not only must *Poskim* always be consulted, but that they also must be brought for on-site inspections of the area and the *eruv* before, during, and after construction. Only thus can the abstract positive attitude be translated into concrete practice. Then *Oneg Shabbos* (the enjoyment of *Shabbos*) will not be enhanced at a cost of diminished *Shemiras Shabbos* (observance of *Shabbos*).

REFERENCES TO SUGYOS IN MESSECHES SHABBOS:

REFERENCES TO SUGYOS IN MESSECHES ERUVIN:

Addenda and Corrigenda

The Contemporary Eruv: Addenda and Corrigenda

Above all, I thank *Hashem Yisborach* for allowing *The Contemporary Eruv* to serve as a vehicle for enhanced study of *Hilchos Eruvin*. I am particularly grateful that He has caused *Talmidei Chachamim* of the highest caliber to take an interest in my work, and to study my *sefer* in detail. Much here has been culled from such material. May *Hashem* reward them for their kindness!

I thank Feldheim Publishers and its wonderful staff for all their kindness and consideration, in the publication of this work and, *b'ezras Hashem*, my forthcoming *sefer* on *Sefer Shoftim* of *Tanach*. I owe a debt of gratitude to Reb Akiva Atwood for his assistance along the way.

Since the first printing, our family has moved to Monsey, New York. May *Hashem* grant my wife, our children, and me, our hearts' fervent desire,

להגדיל תורה ולהאדירה.
Yosef Gavriel Bechhofer
Monsey, NY
11 *Elul* 5762

To Page **IX**:

In the third line, the word should be instructed, not instucted.

To Page **X**:

The last line of the third paragraph should read outstanding illustrations, not illustrations outstanding.

To Pages **18-19**, note **31**:

"The prohibition of carrying without an *eruv* from yard to yard only applies to objects that were or will be inside one of the houses at some point during the course of the ensuing *Shabbos*."

Rabbi Meyer Maryles noted that this is the opinion of the *Chazon Ish, Orach Chaim* (104:28) based on *Tosafos* (*Gittin* 79b, see also *Eruvin* 91a). The *Rashba* (*Eruvin* 91a, *d.h. Yesh Sefarim d'Garsei*), however, is of the opinion that there is no prohibition on carrying objects from yard to yard unless they were in a house when *Shabbos* commenced.

To Page **20**, Fig. **2**:

Rabbi Akiva Yosef Kaplan noted that if the measurements of "2" in the figure represent *tefachim*, as would seem to be the case based on the proportions, then the figure is an incorrect depiction of *parutz k'omed*, as this scenario would be subject to the principle of *lavud*!

To Page **20**, Fig. **3**:

Rabbi Meyer Maryles noted a reference to the *Chazon Ish*, ibid., 68:17.

To Page **21**, note **39**:

Rabbi Akiva Yosef Kaplan, Rabbi Meyer Maryles and Rabbi Zev Kanter noted that the reference should be to the *Bi'ur Halacha* 362:10.

To Page **24**, Note **42**:

See *Mishna Berura* 363:111.

To Page **31**:

"It seems that the *eruv* was never implemented as Rabbi Rosenfeld died shortly after making the proposal."

Rabbi Adam Mintz noted that the statement is incorrect. Rabbi Rosenfeld made his proposal in 1896, and only died on *Rosh Ha'Shana* 1915 (an event reported on the front page of the *St. Louis Globe Dispatch*). Furthermore, an opponent of the *eruv*, Rabbi Shalom Elchanan Jaffe, writes in the introduction to his *Teshuva K'Halacha V'Divrei Shalom* that the rabbi who allowed the *eruv* carried himself, publicly, and instructed one of his *schochtim* to carry on *Shabbos* as well.

To Pages **43-44**:

"*Rashi* states that a *reshus ha'rabbim* is: "...Sixteen *amos* broad. And a city in which there are 600,000 people that has no wall . . . "

Rabbi Meyer Maryles noted a an apparent contradiction between *Rashi* here and *Rashi*, *Eruvin* 47a (*d.h. Shalosh Chatzeiros*) where *Rashi* defines a city that has lost its *reshus ha'rabbim* status as one:

"whose population has diminished to the point that 600,000 people no longer travel in its streets." This seems to indicate that it is not the population of the city that determines whether the streets therein have a *reshus ha'rabbim* status, but rather the amount of people traveling in its streets. (See also *Rashi* to 6b *d.h. Yerushalayim* and *d.h. Abulei d'Mechoza*; 26a *d.h. Arseyasa*; and, 59a *d.h. Ir Shel Yachid*.) Evidently, it is the prevalence of 600,000 people in the city and their travel on its thoroughfares that together cause its major arteries to be considered *reshus ha'rabbim*.

To Page **58**, Note **128** (continued):

Rabbi Meyer Maryles noted that other *Rishonim* who ruled according to Rabbi Yehuda and Rabbi Yochanan include the *Rashba*, *Ritva* and *Milchamos Hashem*, *Eruvin* 22a.

To Page **59**:

"*Me'd'rabbanan*, if any single break in the wall is wider than ten *amos* . . . "

See below, note 134. It should be stressed that although the issue of whether a break more than ten *amos* requires an additional rectification *me'd'orysa* or *me'd'rabbanan* is subject to a dispute, that a rectification <u>is</u> required is a matter of universal agreement!

To Page **60**, Note **133**:

Rabbi Meyer Maryles questioned the proof from the *Tosafos ha'Rosh* to the position of the *Chazon Ish*. Perhaps the *Tosafos ha'Rosh* does

mean that any case of *omed merubeh al ha'parutz* is only *d'rabbanan*, even up to sixteen *amos*. Perhaps he only means that up to each *Tanna*'s respective allowed measurement for the opening of *pasei bira'os* is *d'rabbanan*. That would mean that according to *Rabbanan* up to ten *amos* is *d'rabbanan* but beyond would be *d'orysa*. According to Rabbi Yehuda up to thirteen and a third *amos* would be *d'rabbanan*. Indeed, the *Hashlama*, *Eruvin* 5a, makes such a dichotomy. Furthermore, even if we grant that the *Tosafos ha'Rosh* does mean to that *omed merubeh al ha'parutz* does extend, according to all opinions, to a break of more than ten *amos*, how do we know that it extends to a break of sixteen *amos*?
Nevertheless, we should note that the language of the *Tosafos ha'Rosh* is straightforward and seems to express a universal principle, not one of particular and limited scope and application. (Rabbi Maryles also challenged my assumption that *Rabbeinu Chananel*'s discussion of a break of ten *amos* is relevant to the discussion of *asu rabbim*. To me it seems that since the breaks in the wall of *Yerushalayim* were the phenomenon that rendered it *reshus ha'rabbim* there must be a connection between the character of those breaks and *asu rabbim*.)

To Page **61**, Note **133** (continued):

Concerning the opinion of the *Rashba*, Rabbi Meyer Maryles noted that Rabbi Moshe Feinstein, *Igros Moshe*, *Orach Chaim*, 1:139:5 considers this opinion in his discussion of an *eruv* in Manhattan.

To Page **62**:

"He [the *Chazon Ish*] admits that a *reshus ha'rabbim* does negate an *omed merubeh*, but only where the *reshus ha'rabbim* is *"mefulash,"*...

Rabbi Meyer Maryles noted that the usage of the term *"mefulash"* here is somewhat misleading, as it is evident from Figure 12 that even a street that is *mefulash* will not be a *reshus ha'rabbim* according to the *Chazon Ish* if it is halachically walled in the manner described on pages 62-64.

To Page **65**, Note **134** (continued):

I cited a possible interpretation of *Rashi*, that assumed that the walls surrounding the area he was discussing were not *omed merubeh*. Rabbi Akiva Yosef Kaplan noted that the *Chazon Ish* does not propose this approach in *Rashi*, and that the language of *Rashi* does not seem to support this possibility.

To Page **68**, Note **136**:

The reference should be to note 138, not to note 137.

To Page **68**, Note **137**:

I cited *Sukkah* 5b as the source for the *Halacha l'Moshe me'Sinai* of *tzuras ha'pesach*. Of course, the *Gemara* there generally notes that laws of walls are *Halacha l'Moshe me'Sinai*, but does not explicitly specify that this includes *tzuras ha'pesach*. Rabbi Meyer Maryles noted that although Rabbi Chaim Soloveitchik, *Hilchos Shabbos* 16:16, understands that this is the case, the *Gilyonos Chazon Ish* there questions this assumption.

To Page **69**, Note **138** (continued):

The reference should be to note 159, not to note 22.

To Page **72**, Note **144**:

Rabbi Howard Jachter ("Advice for Proper Eiruv Maintenance," *Chavrusa*, 37:2, p. 5) writes that Rabbi Shlomo Zalman Auerbach told him "that a plumb line should be used but if it is impossible to do so, then eyesight is sufficient." Rabbi Dovid Lifshitz told him "that in the town in Europe where he served as Rabbi (Suwalk) a plumb line was used to measure if the *lechi* was beneath the wire."

To Page **75**:

Both Rabbi Yosef Menachem Mendel Rapoport and Rabbi Meyer Maryles noted that even the *Sha'arei Zion*, who holds the overhead cable may veer away from the imaginary straight line between the *lechayayim*, maintains that one may only carry up to the base of the *lechi* and the imaginary line then drawn from one *lechi* to the next, not up to the actual line of the wire that extends beyond that imaginary boundary.

The difficulty with this resolution is that then each side of the *eruv* would be open to an area in which it is forbidden to carry (*parutz b'milu'o l'makom he'asur lo*, see *Shulchan Aruch*, *Orach Chaim* 360:4)! Rabbi Rapoport conceded the difficulty and noted a similar difficulty raised (concerning very slight deviations, and thus not relevant to the *Shaarei Zion*) and discussed by the *Avnei Nezer*, *Orach Chaim* 295:14-15.

To Page **77**, Note **154**:

I questioned an understanding that the ruling of the *Mishna Berura* invalidating a *lechi* surrounded by fences applies only where those fences surround the *lechi* on all four sides on the basis of *Rashi, Shabbos* 97a-b. Rabbi Yosef Menachem Mendel Rapoport noted that, in fact, the same question may be posed from the language of the *Gemara* itself! Rabbi Rapoport continued to note that the question is posed, on the *Makor Chaim*, the source of the stringency, by *Teshuvos Beis Shlomo, Orach Chaim* 55:5, who, despite the question, writes that the custom is to follow the *Makor Chaim*'s stringency. Rabbi Rapoport also noted that the *Maharsham, Da'as Torah* 363:26 asks the same question on the *Makor Chaim*, and concludes that the *Makor Chaim*'s main concern is not so much with the elimination of the *lechi* by its placement within the confines of a separate *reshus* (the first reason cited by the *Makor Chaim*), but, rather, the lack of *heker* (a readily recognizable rectification) that prevails in such a scenario (his second reason).

To Page **77**, Note **156**:

The reference should be to note 139, not to note 2.

To Page **79**:

"...Every *tzuras ha'pesach* invariably passes over parked cars."

Rabbi Yosef Menachem Mendel Rapoport noted that the *Teshuvos Maharsham, Orach Chaim* 1:207 holds that a *lechi* may be broader than four *amos* (and, for that reason, he allows a *tzuras ha'pesach* to cross over a house). The *Chazon Ish, Yoreh Deah* 172:1, also questions the *Makor Chaim*'s stringency in this area (see below, page 91, note 184).

Rabbi Meyer Maryles questioned whether movable objects - even large ones, such as cars - can be considered true interrupting fences in a *tzuras ha'pesach*.

Rabbi Rapoport noted that the *Avnei Nezer*'s leniency here relies on an additional assumption, viz., that the rectification for the enclosed area need not begin within the first ten *tefachim* from the ground. The *Avnei Nezer* disputes the *Even Ha'Ozer, Orach Chaim* 362, on this point.

Furthermore, noted Rabbi Rapoport, the *Avnei Nezer* must reject the possibility of *gud asek* from the top of the surrounding fence bisecting the *tzuras ha'pesach*. The Avnei Nezer eliminates this potential problem, on the basis of *Tosafos, Sukkah* 17a *d.h. Illu*, who rule that we do not employ *lavud* where its application would lead to a stringency. So too, posits the *Avnei Nezer*, we do not employ *gud asek* where its application would lead to a stringency. The *Rashba, Eruvin* 16b however does employ *lavud* even where it leads to a stringency, and the *Beis Meir, Orach Chaim* 502 holds that even *Tosafos* only state their principle concerning the roof, not concerning the walls of a structure. Other authorities that limit th application of the principle of *Tosafos* include the *Pri Megadim, Orach Chaim, Mishbetzos Zahav* 363:1; *Machatzis Ha'Shekel* 502:9 (explaining the *Magen Avraham* 632:5); and, the *Kehillos Yaakov, Sukkah* 13:8.

To Page **81**, Note **164**:

"The *Chazon Ish*, ibid., 72:1, holds that a *pirtza b'keren zavis* invalidates a *reshus ha'yachid me'd'orysa*."

Rabbi Akiva Yosef Kaplan noted that even the *Chazon Ish* must concede that at least part of the enclosure is a *reshus ha'yachid d'orysa*, as it has three walls. (Furthermore, according to the *Chazon Ish*, even a break of more than ten *amos* only renders an area unenclosed *me'd'rabbanan*.

To Page **82**, Note **167**:

"It appears that there is no need, vis-a-vis the *Rambam*'s opinion, to assess each side independently, and it suffices to have *omed k'parutz* taking the entire perimeter into account."

Both Rabbi Yosef Menachem Mendel Rapoport and Rabbi Avrohom Moshe Seidman questioned this assertion. Rabbi Rapoport noted that the *Maggid Mishne* 16:16 (cited in the *Beis Yosef*, *Orach Chaim*, towards the end of *siman* 362, *d.h. U'Ma She'Kasav u'Bilvad*) seems to hold that each side must be taken independently even according to the *Rambam* (see also *Sha'ar Ha'Tziyun* 363:7). It is not clear, however, that this is, indeed, the portent of the *Maggid Mishne*,

To Page **84**, Note **168** (continued):

The word *tefachim* in the second to last line in the note should be *amos*.

To Page **86**:

"If the poles were within three *tefachim* of the fence, we could probably use *lavud* to validate the *eruv*.

The word probably is superfluous; *lavud* does validate the *eruv*.

To Page **86**, Note **171**:

"...Where the two structures of *omed merubeh* are in line ... "

The language here is not clear. By in line I mean that they are in the form of a continuous wall, with a break in that wall. If the structures are not continuous in that manner, even if they run parallel to each other and are close to one another, *omed merubeh al ha'parutz* does not apply.

To Page **87**, Note **173**:

The reference should be to Figure 27, right-hand side, not to Figure 28.

To Page **88**, Note **177**:

In the first line, there should be a comma between the word Paris and the word Rabbi.

To Page **91**:

See above, addendum to page 79.

To Page **94**, Figure **32**:

Rabbi Yosef Menachem Mendel Rapoport noted that the diagram is incorrect. To employ the principle of *pi tikra* the structure must have two walls adjacent to each other connecting at a corner, not two parallel walls (*Rama, Shulchan Aruch, Orach Chaim* 361:2).

To Page **98**:

"Constructing a *tzuras ha'pesach* around the *karpaf* may accomplish this."

The word may is superfluous. Constructing a *tzuras ha'pesach* does accomplish this.

To Page **99**:

"...This question revolves around the issue of the extent to which the rules and regulations of *eruvin* mimic those of *mezuza*."

Rabbi Meyer Maryles noted that the *Makor Chaim* in his *Tikkun Eruvin* distinguishes between the parameters of *eruvin* and those of *mezuza*. Of course, in terms of *halacha l'ma'aseh* there are significant differences between the two areas - see, for example, the case of a doorway with only one doorpost, on the right side - *Shulchan Aruch, Yoreh De'ah* 287:1 and the *Taz* and *Shach* there.

To Pages **99-100**:

"The *Chazon Ish* and others hold that the parameters are linked."

Rabbi Yosef Menachem Mendel Rapoport noted that those others may include Rabbi Moshe Feinstein, *Igros Moshe*, *Orach Chaim* 1:139:3 in the middle of *d.h. V'Im Ken B'Ha'Gesharim*.

To Page **101**:

"A *mis'asek* is one who commits any forbidden act thinking that is permissible."

Rabbi Akiva Yosef Kaplan noted that it would be more accurate to say:

"A *mis'asek* is one who commits any forbidden act thinking he is doing something else that is permissible.

To Page **101**, Note **207**:

Rabbi Akiva Yosef Kaplan noted that from the discussions of the *Rishonim* in *Eruvin* concerning accidental carrying within an area that is not enclosed in a valid manner, it seems evident that they do not accept the principle that a *shogeg bidi'rabbanan* does not require *Teshuva*.

To Page **103**:

"*Me'd'orysa*, the ownership of an area is not relevant to the prohibition of carrying on *Shabbos* or *Yom Tov*."

Rabbi Meyer Maryles noted the relevant *Tosafos*, *Eruvin* 93b, *d.h.*

Chayav, and the *Rashash* there.

"Pieces of bread ... "

Rabbi Akiva Yosef Kaplan noted that this is incorrect. The bread for the *eruv* must be a whole loaf (albeit, even a small loaf or roll). There was, therefore, a custom to collect flour from all the participants in the *eruvei chatzeiros* and bake a common loaf - see *Shulchan Aruch* and *Rama*, *Orach Chaim* 366:6 (see *Mishna Berura* 366:37 that pieces of bread may not be valid for *eruvei chatzeiros* even *b'di'eved*).

"...The appropriate verbal formula, ... "

Rabbi Meyer Maryles noted that while in *Shulchan Aruch*, *Orach Chaim* 366:15 it is explicit that a verbal formula should accompany the *eruvei chatzeiros*, it is, nevertheless, evident from 366:11 that there are circumstances under which the *eruvei chatzeiros* may be valid even without a verbalization.

To Page **105**, Note **220**:

Rabbi Akiva Yosef Kaplan noted that although it is not necessary to specify that one is renting the right to carry from the non-Jew, it is preferable to specify some right as the subject of the rental.

To Page **106**:

"If, however, only one of the families is *Shomer Shabbos*, then that family utilizes neither *eruvei chatzeiros* nor *sechiras reshus*.

Both Rabbi Akiva Yosef Kaplan and Rabbi Meyer Maryles noted that the incorrect impression is left here that no *sechiras reshus* is necessary. This is corrected later, in note 224, which should probably have appeared here. See *Chiddushei Rabbi Akiva Eiger, Orach Chaim* and *Even ha'Ozer* 385:3, and *Teshuvos Rabbi Akiva Eiger ha'Chadashos siman* 7. See also *Chazon Ish, Orach Chaim* 87:11.

To Pages **108-110**:

"The *Rashba* writes:"

Rabbi Meyer Maryles noted that the impression is created that the concepts under discussion here originate in the *Rashba*. In fact, of course, *tefisas yad* is to be found in *Eruvin* 85b, while the principle that one may rent from an employee or agent is there, 64a.

"They should rent the right to carry throughout the ship from its owner before he distributes the rooms among the other passengers."

Rabbi Akiva Yosef Kaplan noted that the *Rashba*'s language:
"ישכרו מבעל הספינה קודם שיחלקו מקומות ידועים לשוכרים שיוכלו לטלטל בכל הספינה" may be better translated as:

"They should rent from its owner before he distributes the rooms among the other passengers <u>in order that they should be able</u> to carry throughout the ship."

To Page **109**:

"...Or even just the right to place objects on the property, then one may even rent the right to carry from the owner ... "

Rabbi Akiva Yosef Kaplan noted that the *Rashba*'s language: "אלא שיש לו רשות להניח שם שום כלים, שוכרין אפילו מן המשכיר" may be better translated as:

"...Or even just the right to place objects there, then one may even rent from the owner ... "

To Page **110**, Note **231**:

"Nevertheless, Reb Moshe's logic and evidence in this regard are very strong."

Rabbi Akiva Yosef Kaplan noted that the novelty in Reb Moshe's approach is that earlier sources seem to indicate that *tefisas yad* is linked to a right to make use of the premises. While the landlord provides the tenant with appliances, he generally does not have the right to make use of them.

To Page **111**, Note **232**:

"If the owner can evict the tenant any time he pleases, everyone agrees that no further procedures are required."

Rabbi Meyer Maryles noted that the *Chazon Ish, Orach Chaim* 90:31 may not agree with this formulation.

To Page **112**, Note **235**:

Rabbi Yosef Menachem Mendel Rapoport and Rabbi Akiva Yosef Kaplan both brought to my attention the *Teshuvos Rabbi Akiva Eiger* 1:34, where he seems to argue on the *Chavos Yair* and rule that individuals who do not live in the area to be enclosed by an *eruv* do who have the right to travel through the area need not be taken into account - neither in the *eruvei chatzeiros* nor in the *sechiras reshus* (Rabbi Rapoport noted similar positions in the *Rashba*, *Ritva* and *Ran*, *Eruvin* 59b, cited in the *Noda b'Yehuda*, *Tinyana*, *Orach Chaim siman* 39, and cited by the *Sha'arei Teshuva*, *Orach Chaim* 378. It is not clear to me, however, that the circumstances in the *Chavos Yair*'s case and that of Rabbi Akiva Eiger are precisely similar, and the question remains open for discussion: What access (*derisas regel*) is considered an assertion of "ownership," thus requiring *sechiras reshus*; and what access is only considered tantamount to a guest's usage of premises, and thus not generating an obligation of *sechiras reshus*. The ramifications, for an *eruv* between neighbors across a street, or the dwellers on a "dead-end" street, etc. are significant.

To Page **113**, Note **235** (continued):

"...Or, the residents bear responsibility for the maintenance of the sidewalk ... "

Rabbi Akiva Yosef Kaplan noted that this may only suffice according to Rabbi Moshe Feinstein's definition of *tefisas yad* (see above, addendum to page 110, note 231).

To Page **115**, Note 239 (continued):

"...It is entirely possible ... "

Rabbi Akiva Yosef Kaplan noted that this is not just possible, this is, in fact, the case!

To Page **117**:

"Nevertheless, hundreds, perhaps thousands, of *eruvin* have been constructed in urban areas since the time of King Solomon ... "

Rabbi Akiva Yosef Kaplan noted that while this may be true, at the time of the *Gemara* they would collect flour and bake a new loaf of bread for the *eruvei chatzeiros* every week. Thus, the problem raised by the *Chazon Ish* concerning changes in ownership through a year is of more recent origin, only beginning with the advent of the custom to use *matzos* that are replaced only on an annual basis.

Made in the USA